W9-BYK-496

INTERNATIONAL FOLK SONGS

MELODY LINE, CHORDS AND LYRICS
FOR KEYBOARD • GUITAR • VOCAL

HAL•LEONARD®

ISBN 0-7935-7344-0

Visit Hal Leonard on the internet at http://www.halleonard.com

7777 W. BLUEMOUND RD. P.O. BOX 13819 MILWAUKEE, WI 53213

Welcome to the PAPERBACK SONGS SERIES.

Do you play piano, guitar, electronic keyboard, sing or play any instrument for that matter? If so, this handy "pocket tune" book is for you.

The concise, one-line music notation consists of:

MELODY, LYRICS & CHORD SYMBOLS

Whether strumming the chords on guitar, "faking" an arrangement on piano/keyboard or singing the lyrics, these fake book style arrangements can be enjoyed at any experience level — hobbyist to professional.

The musical skills necessary to successfully use this book are minimal. If you play guitar and need some help with chords, a basic chord chart is included at the back of the book.

While playing and singing is the first thing that comes to mind when using this book, it can also serve as a compact, comprehensive reference guide.

However you choose to use this PAPERBACK SONGS SERIES book, by all means have fun!

CONTENTS

Algeria
MA GAZELLE
(My Gazelle)
Moorish Folksong

1. Ah! ah! ma ga - zel - le! ___
2. Ah! ah! ma ga - zel - le! ___
3. Ah! ah! ma ga - zel - le! ___
1. Ah! Ah! my ga - zelle! ___
2. Ah! Ah! my ga - zelle! ___
3. Ah! Ah! my ga - zelle! ___

Ah! c'est la plus bel - le! ___
Ah! c'est la plus bel - le! ___
Ah! c'est la plus bel - le! ___
Ah! come to my sigh - ing. ___
Ah! come to my sigh - ing. ___
Ah! come to my sigh - ing. ___

Sa noi - re pru -
Un seul re - gard
Fath - ma m'en - sor -
Dark eyes glance re -
One bright look she
Fat - ma has en -

nel - le ___ M'a dit a -
d'el - le ___ M'a ren - du
cè - le, ___ Je meurs d'a -
ply - ing ___ With looks of
gave ___ me, ___ And turn'd my
slaved ___ me, ___ And of love

Dm/A A7 Dm/A A

mour, doux a - mour. Viens,
fou, oh! bien fou! Elle
mour, oui, d'a - mour. C'est
love, *looks* *of* *love.* *Come,*
brain *Ah!* *save* *me.* *She's*
I *am* *dy - ing.* *It*

Bb7/A A

bel - le sul - ta - ne, _____ Je t'at -
est si jo - li - e, _____ Que toute
dans la ra - vi - ne, _____ Au - près
I *love* *you* *on - ly,* _____ *'Neath* *the*
so *sweet* *and* *love - ly,* _____ *Ev - 'ry*
was *in* *the* *val - ley,* _____ *Near* *the*

Dm/A A7b9

tends sous le _____ pla - ta - ne Du
al - mé - e en - vi - e, Ses
d'A' in Mas - kou - ti - ne, Qu'el -
fruit *trees* *wait* _____ *I* *lone - ly.* *Ah!*
girl *must* *en - vy* *bear* _____ *her;* *Blue*
vil - lage *Mas - ku - ti - na,* *That*

Dm/A A7 A Em7b5/A A

ren - dez - vous c'est le jour. ⎫
yeux, sa taille et son cou. ⎪
le m'ap - pa - rut un jour. ⎬
fair *one,* *come* *then* *quick - ly,* ⎪
eyes, *and* *neck* *none* *fair - er.* ⎭
she *ap - pear'd* *be - fore* *me.*

Bb7/A

Viens, beau - té char - man - - -
For *the* *day* *is* *dy* - - -

te, Lais - se ta ten - - -
ing, *Soft* *winds* *are* *sigh* - -

te, Voi - ci - le soir,
ing, *Sweet* *is* *the* *night.*

Lais - se _____ ta
Leave _____ *then* _____ *thy*

ten - te, Le ciel est noir, _____
dream - *ing,* *The* *stars* *a* - *bove* _____

Bien _____ noir. _____ Ah!
are _____ *gleam* - *ing.* *Ah!*

ah! ma ga - zel - le! _____ Ah!
Ah! *my* *be* - *lov* - *ed!* _____ *Ah!*

c'est la plus bel - le! _____
come *to* *my* *sigh* - *ing!* _____

Argentina
ARRORO MI NIÑO
(Lullaby, My Baby)

1. Ar - ro - ro mi ni - ño, Ar - ro - ro mi sol,
1. Lul - la - by, my ba - by, Lul - la - by, my sun,

Ar - ro - ro pe - da - zo, de mi cor - a -
Lul - la - by, my sweet - heart, Moth - er's lit - tle

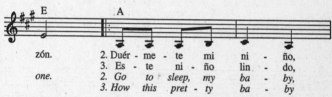

zón. 2. Duér - me - te mi ni - ño,
3. Es - te ni - ño lin - do,
one. 2. Go to sleep, my ba - by,
3. How this pret - ty ba - by

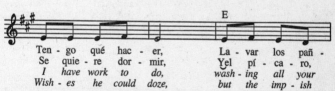

Ten - go qué hac - er, La - var los pañ -
Se quie - re dor - mir, Yel pí - ca - ro,
I have work to do, wash - ing all your
Wish - es he could doze, but the imp - ish

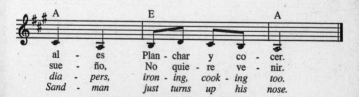

al - es Plan - char y co - cer.
sue - ño, No quie - re ve - nir.
dia - pers, iron - ing, cook - ing too.
Sand - man just turns up his nose.

Australia

BOTANY BAY

1. Fare - well to old Eng - land for - e - ver,
2. There's the cap - tain as is our Com - mand - er,
3. 'Taint leav - in' old Eng - land we cares a - bout,
4. For sev - en long years I'll be stay-ing here,
5. Oh had I the wings of a tur - tle - dove!
6. Now, all my young Doo - kies and Duch-ess - es,

fare - well to my rum culls as well.
there's the bo - 'sun and all the ship's crew.
'taint cos we mis - pels what we knows.
for se - ven long years and a day.
I'd soar on my pin - ions so high.
take warn - ing from what I've to say.

Fare - well to the well known Old Bai - lee
There's the first and sec - ond class pas-sen - gers,
But be - cos all we light fin - gered gen - try
For meet - ing a cove in an a - re - a
Slap bang to the arms of my Pol - ly love,
Mind all is your own as you touch-ess - es,

where I used for to cut such a swell.
knows what we poor con - victs go through.
hops a - round with a log on our toes.
and ta - king his tic - ker a - way.
and in her sweet pres - ence I'd die.
or you'll find us in Bo - tan - y Bay.

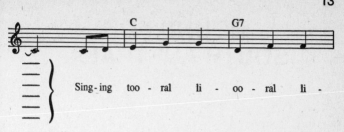

Sing-ing too - ral li - oo - ral li -

ad - di - ty, _____ sing-ing too - ral li -

oo - ral li ay. _____ Sing - ing

too - ral li - oo - ral li - ad - di - ty, _____ sing-ing

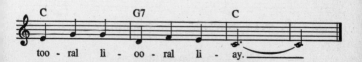

too - ral li - oo - ral li - ay. _____

Australia

BOUND FOR SOUTH AUSTRALIA

Sea Chanty

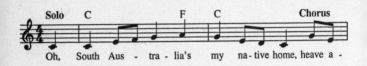

Oh, South Aus - tra - lia's my na - tive home, heave a -

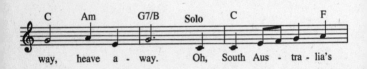

way, heave a - way. Oh, South Aus - tra - lia's

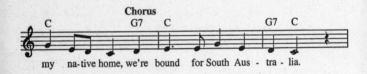

my na - tive home, we're bound for South Aus - tra - lia.

Heave a - way, heave a - way. Oh, heave a - way you

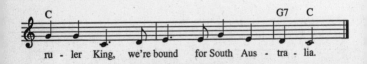

ru - ler King, we're bound for South Aus - tra - lia.

Australia

THE OVERLANDER
(The Queensland Drover)

There's a trade you all know well, it's __

bring- ing cat - tle o - ver. On __ ev -'ry track to the

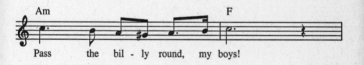

gulf and back, men know the Queens-land dro - ver.

Pass the bil - ly round, my boys!

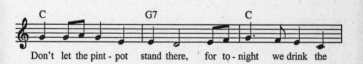

Don't let the pint - pot stand there, for to - night we drink the

health of ev -'ry O - ver - lan - der.

Australia
THE WILD COLONIAL BOY

There was a wild co - lo - nial youth Jack

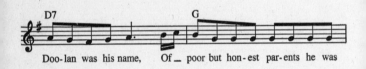

Doo- lan was his name, Of — poor but hon - est par-ents he was

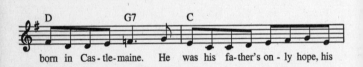

born in Cas-tle-maine. He was his fa-ther's on - ly hope, his

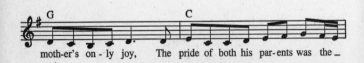

moth-er's on - ly joy, The pride of both his par-ents was the —

wild   co - lo - nial boy.

Chorus

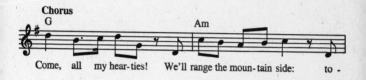

Come, all my hear-ties! We'll range the moun-tain side: to -

ge - ther we will plun-der, to - ge-ther we will ride. We'll

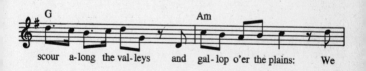

scour a-long the val-leys and gal-lop o'er the plains: We

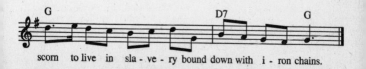

scorn to live in sla - ve - ry bound down with i - ron chains.

Australia

WITH MY SWAG ALL ON MY SHOULDER

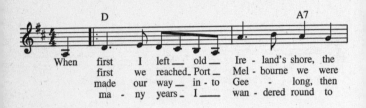

When first I left __ old __ Ire - land's shore, the
first we reached Port __ Mel - bourne we were
made our way in - to Gee - long, then
ma - ny years __ I __ wan - dered round to

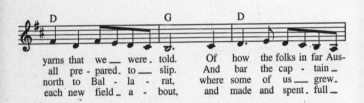

yarns that we __ were told. Of how the folks in far Aus-
all pre - pared to __ slip. And bar the cap - tain __
north to Bal - la - rat, where some of us __ grew __
each new field __ a - bout, and made and spent full __

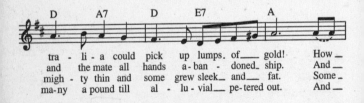

tra - li - a could pick up lumps of __ gold! How __
and the mate all hands a - ban - doned __ ship. And __
migh - ty thin and some grew sleek __ and __ fat. Some __
ma - ny a pound till al - lu - vial __ pe - tered out. And __

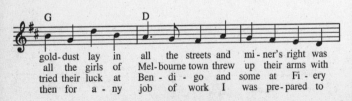

gold - dust lay in all the streets and mi - ner's right was
all the girls of Mel - bourne town threw up their arms with
tried their luck at Ben - di - go and some at Fi - ery
then for a - ny job of work I was pre - pared to

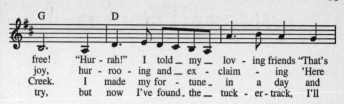

free! "Hur - rah!" I told _ my _ lov - ing friends "That's
joy, hur - roo - ing and _ ex - claim - ing 'Here
Creek. I made my for - tune _ in a day and
try, but now I've found _ the _ tuck - er - track, I'll

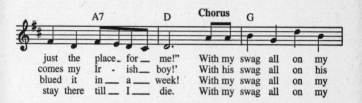

just the place _ for _ me!" With my swag all on my
comes my Ir - ish _ boy!' With his swag all on his
blued it in _ a _ week! With my swag all on my
stay there till _ I _ die. With my swag all on my

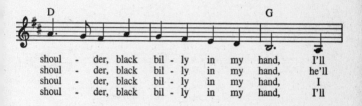

shoul - der, black bil - ly in my hand, I'll
shoul - der, black bil - ly in my hand, he'll
shoul - der, black bil - ly in my hand, I
shoul - der, black bil - ly in my hand, I'll

tra - vel the bush - es of Aus - tra - li - a like a
tra - vel the bush - es of Aus - tra - li - a like a
travel-ed the bush - es of Aus - tra - li - a like a
tra - vel the bush - es of Aus - tra - li - a like a

true - born I - rish - man. When
true - born I - rish - man. We
true - born I - rish - man. For
true - born I - rish - man.

Bahamas
NASSAU BOUND
Sea Chanty

Chorus

1. We sailed on the Sloop John
   up with the John B's
   first mate he _____ got
   Cook - ie he _____ got

B. My grand - fa - ther, and me.
sails, See how the main - sail set.
drunk and broke up the la - dies' trunks. The
fits and throw 'way all the grits.

'Round Nas - sau Town we _____ did
Send for the Cap - tain a - shore, Lem - me go
con - sta - ble he come on board to take him a -
Then he take and throw 'way all the

roam; Drink - in' all night.
home; Oh Sher - iff John - stone
way. Oh Sher - iff John - stone,
corn. Oh Sher - iff John - stone,

Got in - to a fight, I feel so break up,
Won't you let me a - lone I feel so break up,
please let me a - lone I feel so break up,
please let me a - lone. I feel so break up,

D7 ... **G** ... To Coda ⊕

I wan - na go home. ___
I wan - na go home. ___
I wan - na go home. ___
I wan - na go home. ___

Verse
D7 **G**

— There's no bet - ter place than a
— We car - ried ___ la - dies to
— eat a - board the

C **D7**

sail - ing ___ ship, To get an ___ Ed - u -
Nas - sau, ___ Like oth - er ___ sail - ing
Sloop John B., just like the ___ ve - ry

C **G**

ca - tion. You learn to tar the
bo - ats There were twen - ty trunks down
best. ___ But Cook - ie nev - er

C **D7**

rat - lines ___ down, While drink - in' ___ your rum
in the ___ hold, All full of ___ pet - ti
calls it ___ food, he on - ly calls it a

1. - 3.
D.S. al Coda
(4th Chorus)
G **D7**

CODA
⊕

ra - tion. ___ 2. An it's
coats. ___ 3. But the
mess. ___ 4. Then

—

Austria
WERBUNG
(Wooing)

Bosnia
PAUN I KOLO
(Why So Silent, Tell Me, Sweet Bird)

Pa - un pa - se,___ tra - va___ ra - ste,
Why so si - lent,___ tell me,___ sweet bird,

pa - u - ne moj! pa - u - ne
Why so si - lent? Tell me, sweet___ bird,___

moj! pa - u - ne___ moj! Pa - u -
dear, tell me, sweet___ bird___ dear. Are you

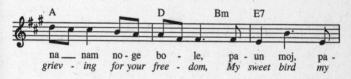

na___ nam no - ge bo - le, pa - un moj, pa -
griev - ing for your free - dom, My sweet bird my

un moj! Pa - u - na___ nam o - ci
sweet bird? Are you long - ing for the

bo - le, pa - un moj pa - un moj!
wood - land, my sweet bird, sweet bird, dear?

Brazil

ROUXINOL DO PICO PRETO
(Nightingale with the Dark Beak)

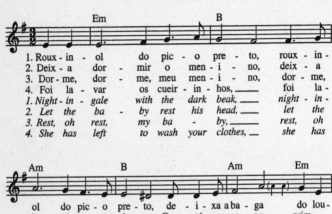

1. Roux - in - ol do pic - o pre - to, roux - in -
2. Deix - a dor - mir o men - i - no, deix - a
3. Dor - me, dor - me, meu men - i - no, dor - me,
4. Foi la - var os cueir - in - hos, ____ foi la -

1. Night - in - gale with the dark beak, ____ night - in -
2. Let the ba - by rest his head, ____ let the
3. Rest, oh rest, my ba - by, ____ rest, oh
4. She has left to wash your clothes, ____ she has

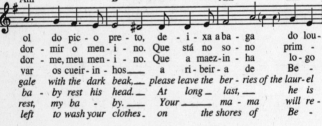

ol do pic - o pre - to, de - i - xa a ba - ga do lou -
dor - mir o men - i - no. Que stá no so - no prim -
var os cueir - in - hos a ri - beir - a de Be -

gale with the dark beak, ____ please leave the ber - ries of the laur - el
ba - by rest his head. ____ At long last, ____ he is
rest, my ba - by. ____ Your ____ ma - ma will re -
left to wash your clothes. on the shores of Be -

eir - o. O o ____ o o! ____
eir - o. O o! ____ O, o! ____
vem. O, o! ____ O, o! ____
lém. O, o! ____ O, o! ____

bush. ____ Oh, oh! ____ Oh, oh! ____
rest - ing. Oh, oh! ____ Oh, oh! ____
turn soon. Oh, oh! ____ Oh, oh! ____
lém. ____ Oh, oh! ____ Oh, oh! ____

Canada

AH! SI MON MOINE VOULAIT DANSER!
(Come and Dance with Me!)

1. Ah! Si mon moi - ne vou - lait dan - ser! Ah!
2. Ah! Si mon moi - ne vou - lait dan - ser! Ah!
3. Ah! Si mon moi - ne vou - lait dan - ser! Ah!
1. Oh! If you come and will dance with me, Oh!
2. Oh! If you come and will dance with me, Oh!
3. Oh! If you come and will dance with me, Oh!

Si mon moi - ne vou - lait dan - ser! Un ca - pu - chon je lui
Si mon moi - ne vou - lait dan - ser! Un froc de bur' je lui
Si mon moi - ne vou - lait dan - ser! Un beau psau - tier je lui
If you come and will dance with me, A love - ly cap I will
If you come and will dance with me, A ging - ham frock I will
If you come and will dance with me, A book of Psalms I will

don - ne - rais, Un ca - pu - chon je lui don - ne - rais.)
don - ne - rais, Un froc de bun' je lui don - ne - rais.)
don - ne - rais, Un beau psau - tier je lui don - ne - rais.)
give to you, A love - ly cap I will give to you.
give to you, A ging - ham frock I will give to you.
give to you, A book of Psalms I will give to you.

Refrain

Dan - se, mon moin', dan - se! Tu n'en - tends pas la
Come, my dear, and dance now! You think you can - not

dan - se, Tu n'en - tends pas mon mou - lin, lon la, Tu
dance now, You think you can - not___ fol - low me, But

n'en - tends pas mon mou - lin mar - cher.
take my hand and___ we will se

Canada
FERRYLAND SEALER
Newfoundland

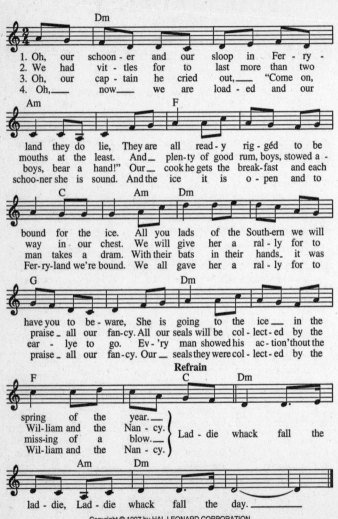

Dm

1. Oh, our schoon-er and our sloop in Fer-ry-
2. We had vit-tles for to last more than two
3. Oh, our cap-tain he cried out,__ "Come on,
4. Oh,__ now__ we are load-ed and our

Am　　　　**F**

land they do lie, They are all read-y rig-géd to be
mouths at the least. And__ plen-ty of good rum, boys, stowed a-
boys, bear a hand!" Our__ cook he gets the break-fast and each
schoo-ner she is sound. And the ice it is o-pen and to

C　　　　**Am**　　**Dm**

bound for the ice. All you lads of the South-ern we will
way in our chest. We will give her a ral-ly for to
man takes a dram. With their bats in their hands__ it was
Fer-ry-land we're bound. We all gave her a ral-ly for to

G　　　　　　　　**Dm**

have you to be-ware, She is going to the ice__ in the
praise__ all our fan-cy. All our seals will be col-lect-ed by the
ear-lye to go. Ev-'ry man showed his ac-tion'thout the
praise__ all our fan-cy. Our__ seals they were col-lect-ed by the

Refrain

F　　　　　　**C**　　**Dm**

spring of the year.__ ⎫
Wil-liam and the Nan-cy.　⎬ Lad-die whack fall the
miss-ing of a blow.__ ⎥
Wil-liam and the Nan-cy. ⎭

Am　　**Dm**

lad-die, Lad-die whack fall the day.

Canada
THE FROG IN THE BOG

Canada
IROQUOIS LULLABY

Ho,   ho, _____   Wa - ta - nay,
Lul - lay, _____   lit - tle one,

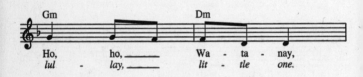

Ho,   ho, _____   Wa - ta - nay,
lul - lay, _____   lit - tle one.

Ho,   ho, _____   Wa - ta - nay,   Ki -
Lul - lay, _____   lit - tle one,   now

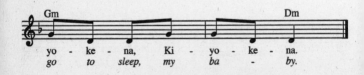

yo - ke - na,   Ki - yo - ke - na.
go to sleep, my ba - by.

Canada

LE MARCHAND DE VELOURS

(The Velvet Merchant)

1. Mon pè-re m'y ma-ri' a-vec un mar-chand de ve-
2. Lepre-mier jour de mesnoc's, ils m'ontjou-é un vi-lain
3. Di-sait dans son lan gag': "Ah! lèv-e-toi, car il est
1. *My fa-thermade me mar-ry one, a vel-vet mer-chant*
2. *First mor-ning of the mar-riage quite a trick was played on*
3. *"Please tell me why a bride should rise be-fore the sun is*

lours, Mon pè-re m'y ma-ri' a-vec un mar-chandde ve-
tour, Le pre-mierjour de mesnoc's, ils m'ontjou-é un vi-lain
jour, Di-sait dans son lan-gag': "Ah! lèv-e-toi, car il est
he. My fa-thermade me mar-ry one, a vel-vet mer-chant
me. First mor-ning of the mar-riage quite a trick was played on
high? Please tell me why a bride should rise be-fore the sun is

lours. Le pre-mier jour de mes noc's, ils m'ont jou-
tour, Je ne fus pas si-tôt cou-ché que l'al-ou-
jour, Faut-il doncqu'un' jeun' ma-ri-é' s'y lève a-
he, The ver-y day of our wed-ding was a
me. I scarce had got-ten in bed when he said,
high?" "The shop is crawl-ing with cus-tom-ers who

Refrain

é un-vi-lain tour,
ett' chan-ta le jour. }Ah! gai lon-la, vi-ve la rou-
vant le pe-tit jour?" }
trick played on__ me.
"Rise, come face the day." }Oh! Sing and dance, tra-la-la-la-
came here to__ buy." }

let-te, Gai lon-la, vi-ve la rou-lé!
ler-a, Sing and__ dance, tra-la-la-la-la.

Chile

MI CABALLO BLANCO
(My White Horse)

Em   Am

1. Es   mi   ca - ba - llo   blan - co,
2. En   a - las deu - na   di - cha
3. Has - ta quea Dios le   pi - do
1. *He's   my   white horse so   hand - some,*
2. *When   hap - py wings trans - port   me,*
3. *I   pray for God's pro - tec - tion:*

B7   Em

Co - moun a - man - e - cer,
Mi   ca - ba - llo   co - rrió,
Que   lo   ten - ga muy   bien,
Shin - ing just like the   dawn.
He   flies a - long so   free,
"Health for my steed pro - vide."

Am   Em

Siem - pre jun - ti - tos   va - mos,
Yen   bra - zos deu - na   pe - na
Sia   su   la - do me   lla - ma,
He   is   a   friend so   faith - ful;
And when my heart is   heav - y,
But when I   go to   heav - en,

B7   Em

Es   mia - mi - go mas   fiel.)
Tam - bién él   me   lle - vó.)
En   mi   blan - qui - toi - ré.)
Bud - dies, we   trav - el   on.)
He   al - ways car - ries   me.)
On   my   white horse I'll   ride.)

Refrain

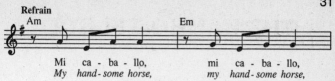

Mi ca - ba - llo, mi ca - ba - llo,
My hand-some horse, my hand-some horse,

gal - o - pan - do va,
gal - lop - ing a - way,

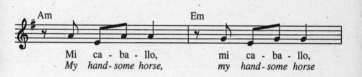

Mi ca - ba - llo, mi ca - ba - llo,
My hand-some horse, my hand-some horse

se vay se va.
rac - es all day.

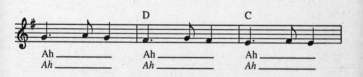

Ah _____ Ah _____ Ah _____
Ah _____ Ah _____ Ah _____

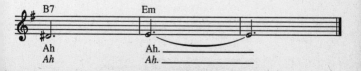

Ah Ah. _____
Ah Ah. _____

China
THE BAMBOO FLUTE

Colombia

DUERME NIÑO PEQUEÑITO
(Sleep, My Baby, Precious Darling)

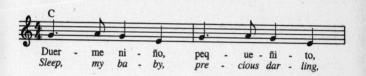

Duer - me ni - ño, peq - ue - ñi - to,
Sleep, my ba - by, pre - cious dar - ling,

Que la no - che vie - ne ya,
For the night is draw - ing nigh,

Duer - me pron - to mo - co - çit - o,
Slum - ber quick - ly, lit - tle ras - cal,

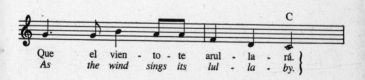

Que el vien - to - te arul - la - rá. }
As the wind sings its lul - la - by. }

Mm mm mm mm Mm mm mm mm mm — mm.

Cuba

GUANTANAMERA

Refrain

E   **A**   **B7**
Guan - ta - na - me - ra   gua - ji - ra
Guan - ta - na - me - ra,   I sing of

E   **A**   **B7**
Guan - ta - na - me - ra
Guan - ta - na - me - ra,

E   **A**   **B7**
Guan - ta - na - me - ra   gua - ji - ra
Guan - ta - na - me - ra,   I sing of

E   **A**   **B7**   **Fine**
Guan - ta - na - me - ra.
Guan - ta - na - me - ra.

1. Yo soy un
2. Mi ver - so es
3. Con los po -
1. I come from
2. My verse is
3. With all the

E   **A**   **B7**
hom - bre sin - ce - ro   de don - de
de un ver - de cla - ro   y de un car -
bres   de la tie - rra   quie - ro yo
where palm trees flou - rish,   to speak the
bright green and shin - ing   and it is
poor   and the hum - ble   I cast my

E / A / B7

cre - ce la pal - ma — Yo soy un
min en - cen - di - do — Mi ver - so es
mi suer - te e - char — Con los po -
truth's my de - si - re. — *I come from*
blood - red and flow - ing. — *My verse is*
fate and de - vo - tion. — *With all the*

E / A / B7

hom - bre sin - ce - ro — de don - de
de un ver - de cla - ro — y de un car -
bres de la tie - rra — quie - ro yo
where palm trees flou - rish, — *to speak the*
bright green and shin - ing — *and it is*
poor and the hum - ble — *I cast my*

E / A / B7

cre - ce la pal - ma — Y an - tes de
min en - cen - di - do — Mi ver - so es
mi suer - te e - char — El a - rro -
truth's my de - si - re. — *And I must*
blood - red and flow - ing: — *A wound - ed*
fate and de - vo - tion. — *The moun - tain*

E / A / B7

mor - rir - me quie - ro, — E - char mis
un cie - rro he - ri - do — Que bus - ca en
yo de la sie - rra — Me com - pla -
sing or I per - ish — *The songs that*
fawn that is go - ing — *In - to the*
streams as they tum - ble — *Mean more to*

E / A / B7 | 1., 2. | 3. B7 — D.C. al Fine

ver - sos del al - ma.
el mon - te am - pa - ro.
ce mas que el mar. __
fill me with fi - re.
hills green and grow - ing.
me than the o - — *cean.*

Congo
KUMBAYA

Kum - ba - ya ya, Kum - ba -
Kum - ba - ya, my Lord, Kum - ba -

ya. Kum - ba - ya ya, Kum - ba -
ya. Kum - ba - ya, my Lord, Kum - ba -

ya, Kum - ba - ya ya, Kum - ba -
ya, Kum - ba - ya, my Lord, Kum - ba -

ya, Ah, ah, Kum - ba - ya.
ya. Oh, Lord, Kum - ba - ya.

Czech Republic

WŠAK NÁM TAK NEBUDE

(Fear Not, O Sweetest One)

Bohemian Folksong and Dance Tune

Wšak __ nám tak ne - bu - de
Fear __ not, O sweet - est one

Až __ se o - že __ nj - me, Wšak nám tak
Fear nei - ther care nor __ woe, Treas - ure I've

ne - bu - de, až se wdá __ me.
hid - den there, Close by the __ stream.

Dá - me sy de - la - ti Ko - ljb - ky
Come to the brook - let __ clear, You should not

na __ dě - ti, Wšak __ nám tak ne - bu - de
have __ to __ fear, Wait then, sweet, joy - ous - ly,

až __ se o - že __ nj - me, Wšak __ nám tak
Mine __ you will sure - ly soon __ be, Fear __ not, O

ne - bu - de, až se wdá __ me.
sweet - est one, Sor - row shall __ flee.

Denmark

HIST, HYOR VEJEN SLÄR EN BUGT
(There, On Down the Road Ahead)
Words by Hans Christian Andersen
Folk Melody

Hist, hyor ve- jen slär en bugt,
There, on down the road a- head,

Lig- ger der et hus så smukt. Væg- gene lidt ___
there's a ti- ny house in red. Crook- ed walls and

skæ- ve stå rud- erne er ___ gan- ske små,
win- dows small, doors that hard- ly close at all.

Dör- en syn- ker halvt i knae, Hun- den göe- r,
Bark- ing dog, he yaps at all, swal- lows chirp and

det lille krae, Un- der ta- get sval- er kvidre
sing for all. And the sun- shine will not last,

sol- en syn- ker- og sa vid're. ___
for the day- light's fa- ding fast. ___

Finland
KEHTO LAULA
(Cradle Song)

1. Pium paum, keh - to heil - ah - taä, Ja
2. Pium paum, viu - lu vin - gah - taä, Ja
3. Pium paum, ker - ran ka - jah - taä, Tuo
1. Ding dong, back and forth it goes; The
2. Ding dong, how the fid - dle plays, And
3. Ding dong, hear the sol - emn peal; The

lap - si vi - a toin - na nuk - ah taä,
nuo - ret kar - ke - loi - hin kii - ruh - taä,
kirk - on kel - lo sul - le il - moit - taä,
cra - dle rocks the child to sleep so soon.
hap - py chil - dren dance now to the tune.
church - 's bell will one day end your toil.

Pium paum Äi - ti lau - laa vain,
Pium paum, nau - ti el - ä - mää
Pois pois hen - ki va - el - taä Ja
Ding dong, while the cra - dle swings,
Ding dong, out the door you go;
On, on, then your soul shall go

Kun sy - dan káp - yán - sa tun - dit - taä.
Sil - lain kun se sul - le hy - my - aä.
ruu - mis mul - lan al - la ma - jan saä.
Moth - er has a lul - la - by to croon.
Life your life, for it is o - ver soon.
While your bod - y sleeps be - neath the soil.

England
THE BANKS OF THE
SWEET PRIMROSES

1. Oh, as I walked out one mid - sum - mer's
2. Are you sad, fair maid, what makes you
3. Stand off, young man, and don't be so de-
4. I will go down to some lone - ly
5. So come all fair maids by me take a

morn - ing, For to view the
wan - der, what is the
ceit - ful, 'tis you that
val - ley, where no man on
warn - ing, and pay at -

fields and the flow - ers so
cause of all your
are the cause of all my
earth there shall me
ten - tion to what I

gay, 'Twas there on the
grief? I will make you as
pain. It is you that has
find. Where the pret - ty lit - tle
say. There is ma - ny a

banks of the sweet prim -
hap - py as a ny
caused my poor heart to
small birds do change their
dark and a cloud - y

England

BLOW THE WIND SOUTHERLY

Words by John Stobbs
Folk Melody

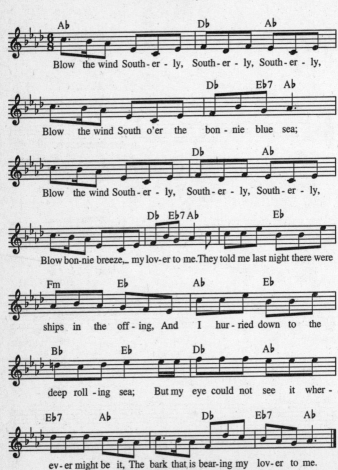

England
COCK ROBIN

1. Who killed Cock Rob-in? ____ I, said the spar-row,
2. Who saw him die? ____ I, said the fly, __
3. Who'll toll the bell? ____ I, said the bull, __
4. Who'll dig his grave? ____ I, said the ow-l,
5. Who'll be the par-son? ____ I, said the rock, __
6. Who'll be chief mourn-er? ____ I, said the dove, __

With my bow and ar-row, I killed Cock Rob-in. ____
With my lit-tle eye, __ I saw him die. ____
Be-cause I can pull, __ I'll toll the bell. ____
With my lit-tle trow-el, I'll dig his grave. ____
With my bell and book, __ I'll be the par-son. ____
I'll mourn for my love, . I'll be chief mourn-er. ____
} All the

birds of the air fell a - sigh-ing and a - sob-bing, When they

heard of the death of poor Cock Rob - in, when they

heard of the death of ____ poor Cock Rob-in. ____

England

THE COASTS OF HIGH BARBARY

Sea Chanty, Sixteenth Century

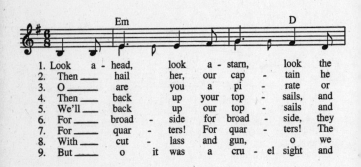

1. Look a - head, look a - starn, look the
2. Then ___ hail her, our cap - tain he
3. O ___ are you a pi - rate or
4. Then ___ back up your top - sails, and
5. We'll ___ back up our top - sails, and
6. For ___ broad - side for broad - side, they
7. For ___ quar - ters! For quar - ters! The
8. With ___ cut - lass and gun, o we
9. But ___ o it was a cru - el sight and

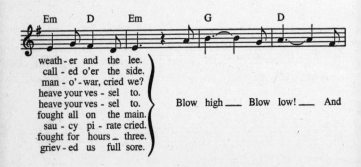

weath - er and the lee.
call - ed o'er the side.
man - o' - war, cried we?
heave your ves - sel to.
heave your ves - sel to.
fought all on the main.
sau - cy pi - rate cried.
fought for hours _ three.
griev - ed us full sore.

Blow high ___ Blow low! ___ And

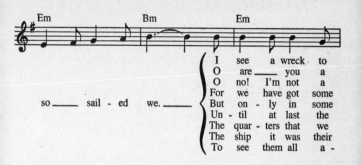

I see a wreck to
O are you a
O no! I'm not a
For we have got some
But on - ly in some
Un - til at last the
The quar - ters that we
The ship it was their
To see them all a -

so ___ sail - ed we. ___

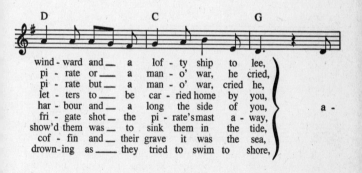

wind - ward and ___ a lof - ty ship to lee,
pi - rate or ___ a man - o' war, he cried,
pi - rate but ___ a man - o' war, cried he,
let - ters to ___ be car - ried home by you,
har - bour and ___ a long the side of you,
fri - gate shot ___ the pi - rate's mast a - way,
show'd them was ___ to sink them in the tide,
cof - fin and ___ their grave it was the sea,
drown - ing as ___ they tried to swim to shore,

a -

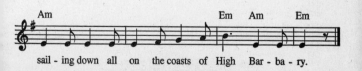

sail - ing down all on the coasts of High Bar - ba - ry.

England
DABBLING IN THE DEW

O where are you go-ing to, my
what is your fa - ther, my
I should chance to kiss ___ you, my
will you be con - stant, my

pret-ty lit-tle dear, with your red ros-y cheeks, and your
pret-ty lit-tle dear, with your red ros-y cheeks, and your
pret-ty lit-tle dear, with your red ros-y cheeks, and your
pret-ty lit-tle dear, with your red ros-y cheeks, and your

coal - black hair? I'm go - ing a - milk - ing, kind
coal - black hair? My fa - ther's a farm - er, kind
coal - black hair? The wind may take it off a-gain, kind
coal - black hair? That I can - not prom-ise you, kind

sir, she an-swer'd me, and it's dab-bling in the dew makes the
sir, she an-swer'd me, and it's dab-bling in the dew makes the
sir, she an-swer'd me, for it's dab-bling in the dew makes the
sir, she an-swer'd me, for it's dab-bling in the dew makes the

milk - maids fair. O
milk - maids fair. And
milk - maids fair. O
milk - maids fair. Then

| Dm | | | C | Bb | Gm | Dm | C |

may I go with you, my pret - ty lit - tle dear, with your
what is your moth - er, my pret - ty lit - tle dear, with your
say, will you mar - ry me, my pret - ty lit - tle dear, with your
I won't mar - ry you, my pret - ty lit - tle dear, with your

| F | | Bb | F/A | Gm | C | F |

red ros - y cheeks, and your coal - black hair? O
red ros - y cheeks, and your coal - black hair? My
red ros - y cheeks, and your coal - black hair? O
red ros - y cheeks, and your coal - black hair?

| Bb | | F | | Dm | | C | *mf* |

you may go with me, kind sir, she an - swered me, for it's
moth - er's a dairy - maid, kind sir, she an - swer'd me, and it's
yes, if you please, kind sir, she an - swer'd me, for it's
No - bod - y ask'd you, kind sir, she an - swer'd me, and it's

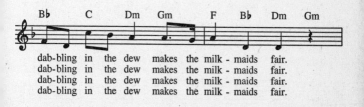

| Bb | C | Dm | Gm | F | Bb | Dm | Gm |

dab - bling in the dew makes the milk - maids fair.
dab - bling in the dew makes the milk - maids fair.
dab - bling in the dew makes the milk - maids fair.
dab - bling in the dew makes the milk - maids fair.

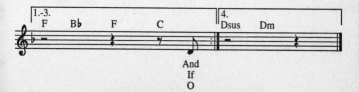

| 1.-3. | | | | 4. | |
| F | Bb | F | C | Dsus | Dm |

And
If
O

England

DIED FOR LOVE

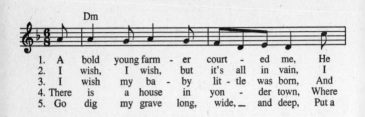

1. A bold young farm - er court - ed me, He
2. I wish, I wish, but it's all in vain, I
3. I wish my ba - by lit - tle was born, And
4. There is a house in yon - der town, Where
5. Go dig my grave long, wide, and deep, Put a

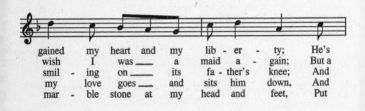

gained my heart and my lib - er - ty; He's
wish I was a maid a - gain; But a
smil - ing on its fa - ther's knee; And
my love goes and sits him down, And
mar - ble stone at my head and feet, Put

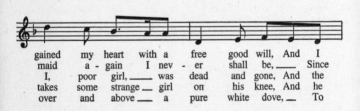

gained my heart with a free good will, And I
maid a - gain I nev - er shall be, Since
I, poor girl, was dead and gone, And the
takes some strange girl on his knee, And he
over and above a pure white dove, To

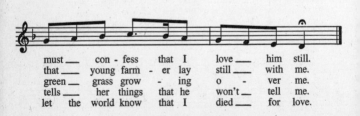

must con - fess that I love him still.
that young farm - er lay still with me.
green grass grow - ing o - ver me.
tells her things that he won't tell me.
let the world know that I died for love.

England
THE GREEN BUSHES

1. As ___ I was a - walk - ing one
2. Oh, ___ why are you loi - ter - ing
3. "I will give you fine bea - vers and
4. I want none of your bea - vers or
5. Come ___ let us be go - ing, kind
6. And ___ when he came there and

morn - ing in May, To hear the birds whis - tle and
here, pret - ty maid?" "I am wait - ing for my true love,"
fine silk - en gowns, I will give you fine pet - ti - coats,
fine silk - en hose, for I'm not so poor as to
sir if you please. Come, let us be go - ing from
found she was gone, he looked ver - y fool - ish, and

see lamb - kins play, I es - pied a young
soft - ly she said. "Shall ___ I be your
flounced to the ground. I will give you fine
mar - ry for clothes. But if you ___ be
un - der these trees. For ___ yon - der is
cried quite for - lorn. "She's ___ gone with a

dam - sel, so sweet - ly sang she, Down ___ by the green
true love, and will you a - gree, down ___ by the green
jew - els, and live but for thee, if you'll leave your own
con - stant and true un - to me, I'll ___ leave my own
com - ing, my true love I see, down ___ by the green
lov - er, and for - sak - en me, and ___ left the green

bush - es, where she chanced to meet me.
bush - es to ___ tar - ry with me.
true love and ___ mar - ry with me.
true love, and ___ mar - ry with me.
bush - es, where he thinks to meet me.
bush - es, where she vowed to meet me.

England

EARLY ONE MORNING

1. Ear - ly one morn - ing, just as the sun was ris - ing, I heard a young maid sing in the val - ley be - low.
2. "Re - mem - ber the vows that you made to me tru - ly. Re - mem - ber how ten - der - ly you nest - led close to me.
3. "Here I now wan - der a - lone as I won - der. Why did you leave me to sigh and com - plain.
4. "How could you slight so a pret - ty girl who loves you, a pret - ty girl who loves you so dear - ly and so warm?
5. "Soon you will meet with an oth - er pret - ty maid - en. Some pret - ty maid - en you'll court her for a - while.
6. Thus sang the maid - en her sor - rows be - wail - ing, thus sang the maid in the val - ley be - low.

"Oh, don't de - ceive ____ me,
Gay is the gar - land,
I ask of the ros - es why should
Though love's ____ fol - ly is
Thus ev - er rang - ing,
"Oh, don't de - ceive ____ me,

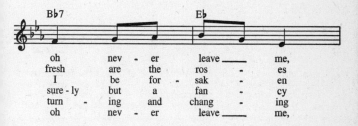

oh nev - er leave ____ me,
fresh are the ros - es
I be for - sak - en
sure - ly but a fan - cy
turn - ing and chang - ing
oh nev - er leave ____ me,

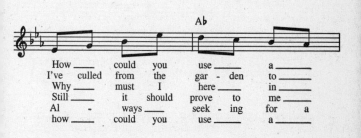

How ____ could you use ____ a ____
I've culled from the gar - den to ____
Why ____ must I here ____ in ____
Still ____ it should prove to me ____
Al - ways ____ seek - ing for a
how ____ could you use ____ a ____

poor ____ maid - en so?"
bind o - ver thee."
sor - row re - main?"
sweet - er than your scorn."
girl ____ that is new."
poor maid - en so?"

England
GREENSLEEVES
Sixteenth Century

1. A - las, my love, __ you do me wrong __ To
2. I have been rea - dy at your hand __ to
3. I bought thee kerch - ers, to thy head, __ that
4. I bought thee pet - ti-coats of the best, __ the
5. Thy gown was of __ the gras - sy green, __ thy
6. Well, I will pray __ to God on high __ that

cast me off __ dis-court-eous-ly; And I have lov - ed
grant what-ev - er you would crave. I have both wag - ed
were wrought fine __ and gal - lant-ly. I kept thee both __ at
cloth so fine __ as fine can be. I gave the jew - els
sleeves of sat - in hang-ing by. Which made thee be __ our
thou my con-stan-cy may - st see. And that yet once be -

you so long, __ De - light - ing in __ your com - pa-ny.
life and land, __ your love - and good - will for to have.
board and bed, __ which cost __ my purse __ well fav - oured-ly.
for thy chest, __ and all __ this cost __ I spent on thee.
har - vest queen, __ and yet __ thou wouldst __ not love __ me.
fore I die __ thou wilt - vouch-safe __ to love __ me.

Refrain

Green - sleeves __ was all my joy, __ Green - sleeves __ was

my de-light; Green - sleeves was my heart of gold, __ And

who but my la - dy Green - sleeves?

England

HARES ON THE MOUNTAIN

Young wom-en, they run like hares on the
wom-en, they sing like birds in the
wom-en, they swim like ducks in the
wom-en, they bloom like lau-rel in
wom-en, they run like hares on the

moun-tain. Young wom-en they run ___ like hares on the
bush-es. Young wom-en they sing ___ like birds in the
wa-ter. Young wom-en they swim ___ like ducks in the
spring-time. Young wom-en they bloom ___ like lau-rel in
moun-tain. Young wom-en they run ___ like hares on the

moun-tain, If I were but a young man I'd soon go a-
bush-es. If I were but a young man I'd go bang them
wa-ter. If I were but a young man I soon would swim
spring-time. If I were but a young man I'd soon go and
moun-tain. If I were but a young man I soon would run

hunt-ing,
bush-es.
af-ter.   } To my right fol-did-dle-de-ro, To my
pluck some.
af-ter.

right fol-did-dle-dee.   { Young   dee.
                          Young
                          Young
                          Young

England

I'M SEVENTEEN COME SUNDAY

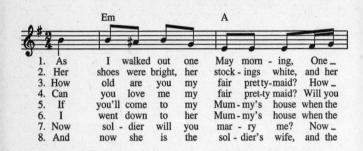

	Em			A		
1. As	I	walked out	one	May morn - ing,	One _
2. Her	shoes were bright,	her	stock - ings	white,	and her
3. How	old are	you	my	fair pret-ty - maid?	How _
4. Can	you love	me	my	fair pret-ty - maid?	Will you
5. If	you'll come	to	my	Mum - my's	house when the
6. I	went down	to	her	Mum - my's	house when the
7. Now	sol - dier	will	you	mar - ry me?	Now _
8. And	now she is	the	sol - dier's wife,	and the

D				Bm		
May	morn - ing	so	ear - ly.	I
buck - les	shone	like	sil - ver.	She
old	are	you	my	hon - ey?	She
mar - ry	me,	my	hon - ey?	She
moon	is	shin - ing	clear - ly.	I
moon	was	bright - ly	shin - ing.	She
is	your	time	of	nev - er.	For
sol - dier	loves	her	dear - ly.	The

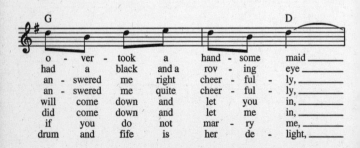

G					D	
o -	ver - took	a	hand - some	maid _____
had	a	black	and a	rov - ing	eye _____
an - swered	me	right	cheer - ful -	ly, _____
an - swered	me	quite	cheer - ful -	ly, _____
will	come	down	and	let	you	in, _____
did	come	down	and	let	me	in, _____
if	you	do	not	mar - ry	me, _____
drum	and	fife	is	her	de -	light, _____

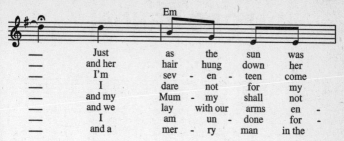

— Just as the sun was
— and her hair hung down her
— I'm sev - en - teen come
— I dare not for my
— and my Mum - my shall not
— and we lay with our arms en -
— I am un - done for -
— and a mer - ry man in the

ris - ing.
shoul - der.
Sun - day.
Mum - my.
hear - me. } With my rue dum day,
twin - ing.
ev - er.
morn - ing.

fol the did - dle dol   Fol the dol the

did - dle dum the day. ____

England

LORD RENDAL

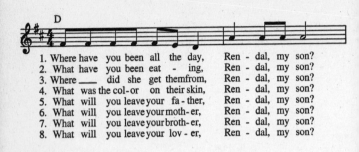

1. Where have you been all the day, Ren - dal, my son?
2. What have you been eat - ing, Ren - dal, my son?
3. Where ___ did she get them from, Ren - dal, my son?
4. What was the col - or on their skin, Ren - dal, my son?
5. What will you leave your fa - ther, Ren - dal, my son?
6. What will you leave your moth - er, Ren - dal, my son?
7. What will you leave your broth - er, Ren - dal, my son?
8. What will you leave your lov - er, Ren - dal, my son?

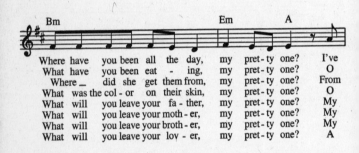

Where have you been all the day, my pret - ty one? I've
What have you been eat - ing, my pret - ty one? O
Where ___ did she get them from, my pret - ty one? From
What was the col - or on their skin, my pret - ty one? O
What will you leave your fa - ther, my pret - ty one? My
What will you leave your moth - er, my pret - ty one? My
What will you leave your broth - er, my pret - ty one? My
What will you leave your lov - er, my pret - ty one? A

been to my sweet - heart, moth - er, I've
eels and ___ eel broth, moth - er, O
hed - ges and ditch - es, moth - er, From
spick - it and spark - it moth - er, O
land and ___ hous - es moth - er, my
gold and ___ sil - ver moth - er, my
cows and ___ hors - es moth - er, my
rope to ___ hang her, moth - er, a

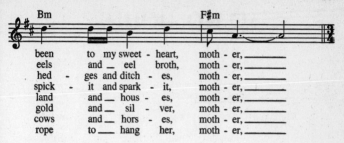

been   to my sweet - heart,   moth - er, _____
eels   and _ eel   broth,   moth - er, _____
hed - ges and ditch - es,   moth - er, _____
spick - it and spark - it,   moth - er, _____
land   and _ hous - es,   moth - er, _____
gold   and _ sil - ver,   moth - er, _____
cows   and _ hors - es,   moth - er, _____
rope   to _ hang her,   moth - er, _____

Refrain

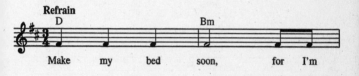

Make   my   bed   soon,   for I'm

sick   to   my   heart   and   I

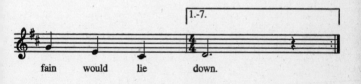

1.-7.

fain   would   lie   down.

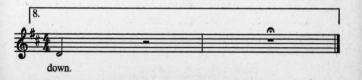

8.

down.

England

O NO, JOHN!

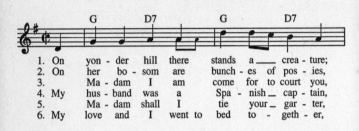

1. On yon-der hill there stands a ___ crea-ture;
2. On her bo-som are bunch-es of pos-ies,
3. Ma-dam I am come for to court you,
4. My hus-band was a Spa-nish cap-tain,
5. Ma-dam shall I tie your ___ gar-ter,
6. My love and I went to bed to-geth-er,

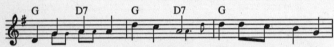

Who she is I do not know. I'll go and court her
on her breast where flow-ers grow. If I should chance to
if your fa-vor I can gain. If you ___ will but
went to sea a month; a-go. The ver-y last time we
tie it a lit-tle a-bove your knee? If my hand should slip a
there we lay till cocks did crow. Un-close your arms my

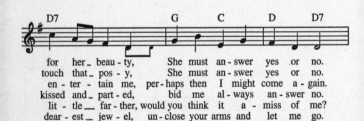

for her ___ beau-ty, She must an-swer yes or no.
touch that ___ pos-y, She must an-swer yes or no.
en-ter-tain me, per-haps then I might come a-gain.
kissed and ___ part-ed, bid me al-ways an-swer no.
lit-tle ___ far-ther, would you think it a-miss of me?
dear-est ___ jew-el, un-close your arms and let me go.

O no, John! No, John! No, ___ John! No!

England
O WALY, WALY

1. The wa - ter is wide, I can - not get o'er And nei - ther have I wings to fly. O go and get me some lit - tle boat To car - ry o'er my true love and I.

2. I put my hand in - to one soft bush, think - ing the sweet - est flow'r to find. I prick'd my fin - ger to the bone, and left the sweet - est flow'r a - lone.

3. I leaned my back up a - gainst some oak, think - ing it was a trust - y tree. But first he bend - ed and then he broke, so did my love prove false to me.

4. Must I be bound, O, and he go free, must I love one that don't love me! Why should I act such a child - ish part, and love a man that will break my heart.

5. O love is hand - some and love is fine, and love is charm - ing when it is true. As it grows old - er it grow - eth cold - er and fades a - way like the morn - ing dew.

England

THE OAK AND THE ASH

Seventeenth Century

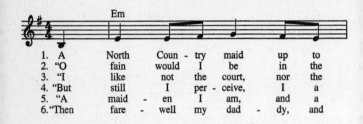

1. A   North   Coun - try   maid   up   to
2. "O   fain   would   I   be   in   the
3. "I   like   not   the   court,   nor   the
4. "But   still   I   per - ceive,   I   a
5. "A   maid - en   I   am,   and   a
6. "Then   fare - well   my   dad - dy,   and

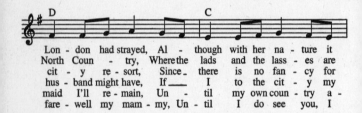

Lon - don had strayed, Al - though with her na - ture it
North Coun - try, Where the lads and the lass - es are
cit - y re - sort, Since there is no fan - cy for
hus - band might have, If I to the cit - y my
maid I'll re - main, Un - til my own coun - try a -
fare - well my mam - my, Un - til I do see you, I

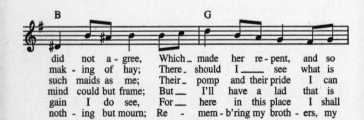

did not a - gree, Which made her re - pent, and so
mak - ing of hay; There should I see what is
such maids as me; Their pomp and their pride I can
mind could but frame; But I'll have a lad that is
gain I do see, For here in this place I shall
noth - ing but mourn; Re - mem - b'ring my broth - ers, my

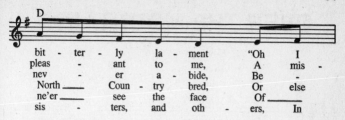

bit - ter - ly	la - ment	"Oh	I
pleas - ant	to	me,	A	mis -
nev - er	a - bide,	Be -
North ___ Coun - try	bred,	Or	else
ne'er ___ see	the	face	Of ___
sis - ters,	and	oth - ers,	In

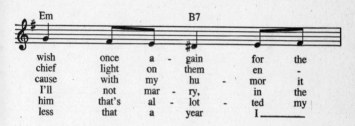

wish	once	a - gain	for	the
chief	light	on	them	en -
cause	with	my	hu - mor	it
I'll	not	mar - ry,	in	the
him	that's	al - lot - ted	my
less	that	a	year	I ___

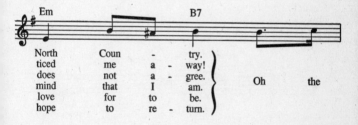

North	Coun - try. }
ticed	me a - way! }
does	not a - gree. }
mind	that I am. } Oh	the
love	for to be. }
hope	to re - turn. }

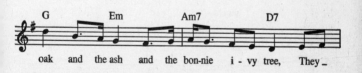

oak and the ash and the bon-nie i - vy tree, They _

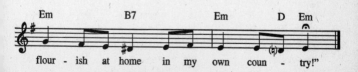

flour - ish at home in my own coun - try!"

England

OVER THE MOUNTAINS
(Love Will Find Out the Way)
Seventeenth Century

1. O - ver the ___ moun - tains And ___
2. When there is ___ no place For the
3. You may es - teem him A ___
4. Some think to ___ lose him By ___
5. If earth it should part him, He would
6. There is no ___ striv - ing To ___

o - ver the waves,
glow - worm to lie,
child ___ for his might;
hav - ing him con - fined,
gal - lop it o'er;
cross ___ his in - tent;

Un - der the ___ foun - tains And ___
When there is ___ no space For re -
Or you may deem him A ___
And some do sup - pose him, Poor ___
If seas should o'er - thwart him, He would
There is no con - triv - ing His ___

un - der the graves; Un - der
ceipt ___ of a fly; When the
cow - ard for his flight; But if
heart! ___ to be blind; But if
swim ___ to the shore; Should his
plots ___ to pre - vent; But if

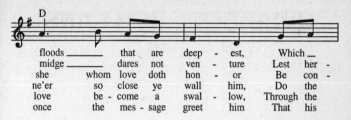

D

floods _____ that are deep - est, Which _
midge _____ dares not ven - ture Lest her -
she whom love doth hon - or Be con -
ne'er so close ye wall him, Do the
love be - come a swal - low, Through the
once the mes - sage greet him That his

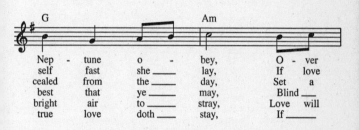

G   Am

Nep - tune o - bey, O - ver
self fast she ____ lay, If love
cealed from the ____ day, Set a
best that ye ____ may, Blind _
bright air to ____ stray, Love will
true love doth ____ stay, If ____

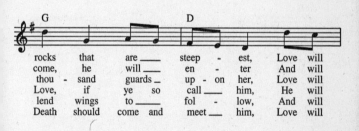

G   D

rocks that are ____ steep - est, Love will
come, he will ____ en - ter And will
thou - sand guards _ up - on her, Love will
Love, if ye so call ____ him, He will
lend wings to ____ fol - low, And will
Death should come and meet ____ him, Love will

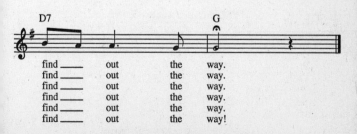

D7   G

find ____ out the way.
find ____ out the way.
find ____ out the way.
find ____ out the way.
find ____ out the way.
find ____ out the way!

England

SCARBOROUGH FAIR

1. Where are you go - ing? To Scar - bo-rough Fair?
2. Tell her to make me a cam - bric shirt,
3. Tell her to wash it in yon - der well,
4. Tell her to plough me an a - cre of land,
5. Tell her to plough it with one ram's horn,
6. Tell her to reap it with a sick - le of leath - er,
7. Tell her to gath - er it all in a sack,

Pars - ley, sage, rose - mar - y and thyme, Re -
Pars - ley, sage, rose - mar - y and thyme, With
Pars - ley, sage, rose - mar - y and thyme, Where
Pars - ley, sage, rose - mar - y and thyme, Be -
Pars - ley, sage, rose - mar - y and thyme, And
Pars - ley, sage, rose - mar - y and thyme, And
Pars - ley, sage, rose - mar - y and thyme, And

mem - ber me to a bon - ny lass there, For
out an - y nee - dle or thread work'd in it, and
wa - ter ne'er sprung nor a drop of rain fell, and
tween the sea and the salt sea strand, and
sow it all o - ver with one pep - per - corn, and
tie it all up with a tom - tit's feath - er, and
car - ry it home on a but - ter - fly's back, and

once she was a true lov - er of mine.
she shall be a true lov - er of mine.
she shall be a true lov - er of mine.
she shall be a true lov - er of mine.
she shall be a true lov - er of mine.
she shall be a true lov - er of mine.
she shall be a true lov - er of mine.

England

SUMER IS ICUMEN IN

(Summer Is A-Coming In)

Thirteenth Century

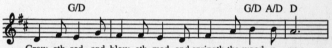

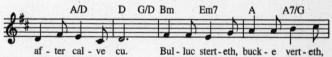

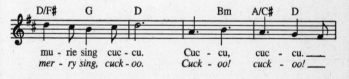

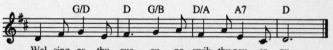

England

THE TREES ARE GETTING HIGH

Eighteenth Century

1. The trees are get-ting high, and the leaves are grow-ing
2. It's moth - er, dear moth - er, you've done to me much
3. It's daugh - ter, dear daugh - ter, I've done to ye no
4. It's moth - er, dear moth - er, and if it pleas - es
5. So at the age of thir - teen he was a mar - ried

green, The time has gone and past my love that
wrong, You've mar - ried me to a bon - ny boy, his
wrong, I've mar - ried ye to a bon - ny boy, he
you, We'll send him to the col - lege for an -
man, And at the age of four - teen the

you and I have seen; 'Twas on a win - ter's
age it is so young; His age is on - ly
is some rich lord's son; A la - dy he will
oth - er year or two; And all a - round his
fa - ther of a son, And at the age of

eve - ning as I sat all a - lone, There I
twelve, my - self scare - ly thir - teen, Say-ing
make you, if a la - dy you'll be made, Say-ing
arm we'll tie a rib - bon blue, And
fif - teen his grave was grow - ing green, And

spied a bon - ny boy, young but grow - ing.
your bonny boy is young but he's grow - ing.
your bonny boy is young but he's grow - ing.
that will be a to - ken that he's mar - ried.
that put an end to his grow - ing.

England

WEEL MAY THE KEEL ROW

Eighteenth Century

1. As I came thro' Sand - gate, Thro' Sand - gate, thro' Sand - gate, As I came thro' Sand - gate, I heard a las - sie sing: "O, weel may the keel row, The keel row, the keel row, O, weel may the keel row That my lad-die's in."

2. "O wha's like my John - nie, Sae lithe, sae blithe, sae bon - nie? He's foremost 'mang the mon - y keel lads o' coal - y Tyne: He'll set or row sae tight - ly, Or, in the dance sae spright - ly, He'll cut and shuf - fle slight - ly, 'Tis true, were he not mine."

3. "He wears a blue bon - net, Blue bon - net, blue bon - net; He wears a blue bon - net, A dim - ple in his chin; And weel may the keel row, The keel row, the keel row, And weel may the keel row, That my lad-die's in."

England

WHEN COCKLESHELLS
TURN SILVERBELLS

Seventeenth Century

When cock - le - shells _____ turn sil - ver - bells,
O had I wist _____ be - fore I

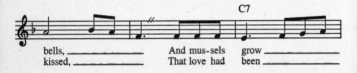

bells, _____ And mus - sels grow _____
kissed, _____ That love had been _____

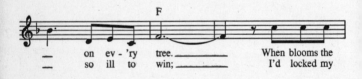

__ on ev - 'ry tree. _____ When blooms the
__ so ill to win; _____ I'd locked my

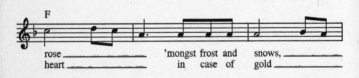

rose _____ 'mongst frost and snows, _____
heart _____ in case of gold _____

__ Then will my false _____ love prove true to
__ And pinned it with _____ a sil - ver

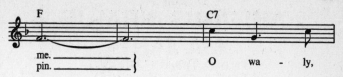

70

France

AH! VOUS DIRAI-JE, MAMAN?

(Twinkle, Twinkle, Little Star)

French Words and Melody, 1761
English Words by Jane Taylor, 1806

1. Ah! vous di - rai - je, ma - man,
1. Oh! dear ma - ma, shall I say
(Twin - kle, twin - kle, lit - tle star,
2.,3. *(See additional lyrics)*

Ce qui cau - se mon tour - ment?
what tor - ments me night and day?
how I won - der what you are,

De - puis que j'ai vu Li - san - dre
Since the time I saw Ly - san - der,
Up a - bove the world so high

Me re - gar - der d'un oeil ten - dre
And I saw his look so ten - der,
Like a dia - mond in the sky.

*Traditional English lyric; it is not, however, a translation of the Original French words.

Mon coeur dit à chaque ins - tant:
My heart tells me ev - 'ry hour
Twin - kle, twin - kle lit - tle star,

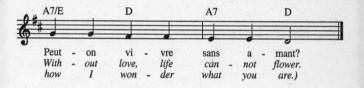

Peut - on vi - vre sans a - mant?
With - out love, life can - not flower.
how I won - der what you are.)

Additional Lyrics

2. L'autre jour dans un bosquet,
De fleurs il fit un bouquet;
Il en para ma houlette
Me disant: "Chère brunette,
Flore est moins belle que toi,
L'amour moins tendre que moi."

3. Je rougis et par malheur
Un soupir trahit mon coeur;
Le cruel, avec adresse,
Profita de ma faiblesse.
Hélas! maman, un faux pas
Me fit tomber dans ses bras.

2. It was just the other day,
That he brought me a bouquet;
He was really very charming
And he said to me: "My darling,
No girl can compare with you,
And I swear my love to you.

3. How I blushed! And, sad to say,
Sighing gave my heart away.
My poor heart with love was reeling
And I could not hide my feeling;
Then alas! Mama, his charms
Led me straight into his arms.

France

AUPRÈS DE MA BLONDE

(Nearby to My Dear One)

G

1. Dans les jar-dins d'mon pè-re, Les
1. Now in my fa-ther's gar-den The

2.- 6. *(See additional lyrics)*

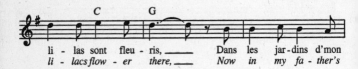

C   G

li-las sont fleu-ris,_____ Dans les jar-dins d'mon
li-lacs flow-er there,_____ Now in my fa-ther's

C   G

pè-re, Les li-las sont fleu-ris,_____ Tous
gar-den, The li-lacs flow-er there,_____ The

E7   Am   D7

les oi-seaux du mon-de Vienn't y fai-re leurs
birds from all the earth are en-chant-ing in the

G

nids,_____ Au-près de ma blon-de,
air._____ Near-by to my dear one,

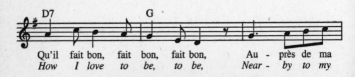

D7   G

Qu'il fait bon, fait bon, fait bon, Au-près de ma
How I love to be, to be, Near-by to my

blon - de,   Qu'il fait bon   dor - mir. _____
dear   one .   how   I   love   to   be. _____

Additional Lyrics

2. La caill', la tourterelle,
   Et la jolie perdrix,
   La caill', la tourterelle,
   Et la jolie perdrix,
   Et ma jolie colombe
   Qui chante jour et nuit.
   Refrain

2. The quail, the grey woodpigeon,
   And speckled partridge come,
   The quail, the grey woodpigeon,
   And speckled partridge come,
   My little dove, my dearest,
   That night and day doth croon.
   Refrain

3. Qui chante pour les filles
   Qui n'ont pas de mari,
   Qui chante pour les filles
   Qui n'ont/pas de mari.
   Pour moi, ne chante guère,
   Car j'en ai un joli,
   Refrain

3. It's comforting the maidens
   Unmarried and alone,
   It's comforting the maidens,
   Unmarried and alone.
   Sweet dove, don't sing for me then,
   A man, I have my own.
   Refrain

4. Dites-nous donc, la belle,
   Où donc est vot' mari?
   Dites-nous donc, la belle,
   Où donc est vot' mari?
   Il est dans la Hollande,
   Les Hollandais l'ont pris,
   Refrain

4. O tell us, tell us lady,
   Where is your husband gone?
   O tell us, tell us lady
   Where is your husband gone?
   In Holland he's a prisoner,
   The Dutch have taken him.
   Refrain

5. Que donneriez-vous, belle,
   Pour avoir votre ami?
   Que donneriez-vous, belle,
   Pour avoir votre ami?
   Je donnerais Versailles,
   Paris et Saint-Denis,
   Refrain

5. What would you give, my beauty,
   To have your husband home?
   What would you give, my beauty,
   To have your husband home?
   Versailles I'd gladly give them,
   And Paris and Notre Dame.
   Refrain

6. Je donnerais Versailles,
   Paris et Saint-Denis,
   Je donnerais Versailles,
   Paris et Saint-Denis,
   Les tours de Notre-Dame,
   Et l'clocher d'mon pays;
   Refrain

6. Versailles I'd gladly give them,
   And Paris and Notre Dame;
   Versailles I'd gladly give them,
   And Paris and Notre Dame,
   Saint Denis's Cathedral,
   And our church-spire at home.
   Refrain

France

FRÈRE JACQUES
(Are You Sleeping?)

Frè – re Jac – ques, Frè – re
Are you sleep – ing? Are you

Jac – ques, Dor – mez – vous?
sleep – ing? Broth – er John,

Dor – mez – vous? son – nez les ma –
Broth – er John, morn – ing bells are

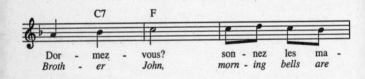

ti – nes, son – nez les ma – ti – nes:
ring – ing, morn – ing bells are ring – ing:

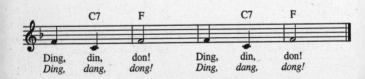

Ding, din, don! Ding, din, don!
Ding, dang, dong! Ding, dang, dong!

France

LA FILLE DE LA MEUNIÈRE
(The Miller's Daughter)
Auvergne

C'est la fill' de la Meu- nièr- e Qui dan -
There she goes, the Mil- ler's daugh- ter, Who is

se a- vec Tho- mas. Elle a per- du sa jarre-
danc- ing there with Tom. You can see she's lost her

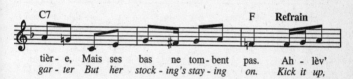

tièr- e, Mais ses bas ne tom- bent pas. Ah- lèv'
gar- ter But her stock- ing's stay- ing on. Kick it up,

donc, lèv' donc la gi- gue, Ah lèv'
kick it up, kick it up, high- er. Kick it up,

donc, lèv' donc plus haut. Ah lèv' donc, lèv' donc la
kick it up, kick it up high. Kick it up, kick it up, kick it up,

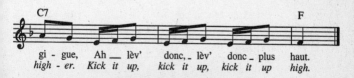

gi- gue, Ah lèv' donc, lèv' donc plus haut.
high- er. Kick it up, kick it up, kick it up high.

France

PASSANT PAR PARIS

(On the Paris Way)

Sea Chanty, Eighteenth Century

1. Pas - sant par Pa - ris, Vi - dant la bou -
2. Jean, prends garde à toi, L'on cour - tis' ta
3. J'ai eu de son coeur La fleur la plus

1. *On the Pa - ris way, Drink - ing all the*
2. *"John, look out, look out, Some - one's got your*
3. *She gave me her heart, None can take my*

teil - le, Pas-sant par Pa - ris, Vi - dant la bou -
bel - le: Jeanprends garde à toi, L'oncour-tis' ta
bel - le, J'ai eu de son coeur La fleur la plus

way there, On the Pa - ris way, drink-ing all the
girl there, John, go home right now, some-one'sgot your
place there, She gave me her heart, None can take my

teil - le, Un de mes a - mis, me dit à l'o
bel - le: Cour-tis' qui vou - dra, Je me moqu' bien
bel - le. Dans un grand lit blanc Gré - é de den -

way there, Saw a pal from home, he had lots to
girl there. I say, let it be, want no more of
place there. In our big white bed, o - ver-hung with

Refrain

reil - le.
del - le." } Bon, bon, bon, Le bon
tel - les.

say there.
her there. } Hey, hey, hey, Give me
lace there.

vin   m'en - dort, L'a-mour me ré - veil - le, Le bon
wine   to   sleep, Love will wake me ear - ly, Give me

vin   m'en - dort, _____   L'a - mour
wine   to   sleep, _____   Love will

me   ré - veille   en -   core.
wake   me   up   a -   gain.

Additional Lyrics

4. J'ai eu trois garçons,
   Tous trois capitaines,
   J'ai eu trois garçons
   Tous trois capitaines,
   L'un est à Bordeaux,
   L'autre à La Rochelle,
   Refrain

5. L'troisième à Paris,
   Qui f'ra comm' son père,
   L'troisième à Paris,
   Qui f'ra comm' son père,
   Ira d'ville en bourg,
   Toujours buvant bouteille,
   Refrain

4. *She gave me three sons,*
   Captains one and all-o
   She gave me three sons,
   Captains one and all-o,
   At Bordeaux there's one,
   One at La Rochelle-o,
   Refrain

5. *And the youngest there,*
   Through the world does stray-o,
   And the youngest there,
   Through the world does stray-o,
   Like his father here,
   Drinking all the way-o,
   Refrain

Germany
ACH DU LIEBER AUGUSTIN
(O My Dearest Augustine)
Eighteenth Century

1. Ach du lie - ber Au - gu - stin,
2. Ach du lie - ber Au - gu - stin,
1. O my dear - est Au - gus - tine,
2. O my dear - est Au - gus - tine,

Au - gu - stin Au - gu - stin,
al - les ist hin!
Au - gus - tine, Au - gus - tine,
ev - 'ry - thing's gone!

Geld ist weg, Mad'l ist weg, al - les weg,
Mon - ey's gone, girls are gone, ev - 'ry - thing!

al - les weg! Ach du lie - ber
ev - 'ry - thing! O my dear - est

Au - gu - stin, al - les ist hin.
Au - gus - tine, ev - 'ry - thing's gone.

Germany

DREI LILIEN
(Three Lilies)

Drei Li - li - en, drei Li - li - en, die
Three lil - ies, three lil - ies, I

pflanzt' ich auf mein Grab, da
plant - ed on my tomb, then

kam ein stol - zer Rei - ter und brach si
came a horse - man proud and broke off each

ab. Ju - vi - val - le-ral - le-ral - le-ral - le -
bloom. Ju - vi - val - le-ral - le-ral - le-ral - le-

ra, ju - vi - val - le-ral - le-ral - le-ral - le -
ra, ju - vi - val - le-ral - le-ral - le-ral - le-

ra, da kam ein stol - zer
ra, then came a horse - man

Rei - ter und brach sie ab.
proud and broke off each bloom.

Germany

DIE SCHNITZELBANK
(The Carving Bench)

Tutti

Ei du schö - ne, ei du schö - ne,
O you love - ly, O you love - ly,

ei du schö - ne Schnit - zel - bank.
O you love - ly carv - ing bench.

Solo

1. Ist das nicht ein - e Schnit - zel - bank?
2. Ist das nicht ein ___ Hin und Her?
3. Ist das nicht ein ___ Krumm und Grad?
1. Is - n't that a ___ carv - ing bench?
2. Is - n't that an ___ up and down?
3. Is - n't that a ___ bend and kneel?

Tutti

Ja das ist ein - e Schnit - zel - bank.
Ja das ist ein ___ Hin und Her.
Ja das ist ein ___ Krumm und Grad.
Yes that is a ___ carv - ing bench.
Yes that is an ___ up and down.
Yes that is a ___ bend and kneel.

Solo

Ist das nicht ein Kurz und Lang?
Ist das nicht 'ne Licht - putz - scher?
Ist das nicht ein Wag - en - rad?
Is - n't that a Swiss and French?
Is - n't that an an - gel's crown?
Is - n't that a wag - on wheel?

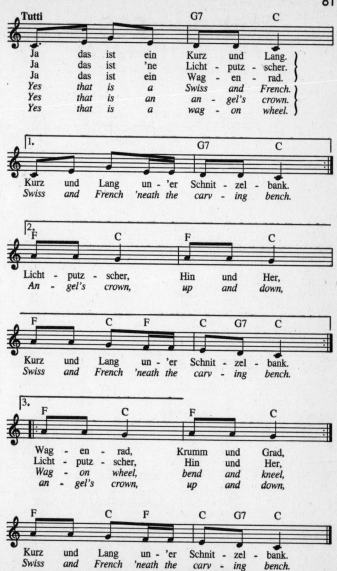

Germany

DU, DU LIEGST MIR IM HERZEN

(You, You Weigh on My Heart)

weißt	nicht,	wie	gut	ich	dir	bin.
fühl'	ich	al -	lein	nur	für	dich.
daß	uns	die	Lie -	be	ver -	eint.
don't	*you*	*know*	*I*	*would*	*be*	*kind.*
such	*sweet*	*af -*	*fec -*	*tion*	*you'll*	*see.*
wed	*me!*	*How*	*glad*	*I*	*would*	*be.*

Ja,	ja
Ja,	ja
Ja,	ja
Yes,	*yes*
Yes,	*yes*
Yes,	*yes*

ja,	ja,	weißt	nicht,	wie
ja,	ja,	fühl'	ich	al -
ja,	ja,	daß	uns	die
yes,	*yes,*	*don't*	*you*	*know*
yes,	*yes,*	*such*	*sweet*	*af -*
yes,	*yes,*	*wed*	*me!*	*How*

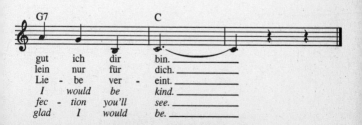

gut	ich	dir	bin.
lein	nur	für	dich.
Lie -	be	ver -	eint.
I	*would*	*be*	*kind.*
fec -	*tion*	*you'll*	*see.*
glad	*I*	*would*	*be.*

Germany

EIN PROSIT DER GEMÜTLICHKEIT

(To All Good Cheer)

Drinking Song

Ein Pro - sit, ein Pro - sit der Ge -
A *toast* *now,* *a* *toast* *now,* *and to*

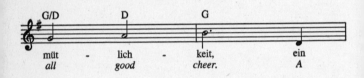

müt - lich - keit, ein
all *good* *cheer.* *A*

Pro - sit, ein Pro - sit der Ge -
toast *now,* *a* *toast* *now,* *and to*

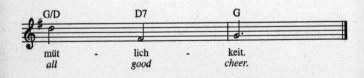

müt - lich - keit.
all *good* *cheer.*

Germany
GAUDEAMUS IGITUR
(Let Us All Be Joyful Now)
Student Drinking Song

Gau - de - a - mus i - gi - tur
Let us all be joy - ful now

ju - ve - nes dum su - mus
while we're young and full of life.

Post ju - cun - dam ju - ven - tu - tem
Af - ter youth has run its dis - tance,

post mo - les - tam se - nec - tu - tem,
at the end of our ex - is - tence,

Nos ha - be - bit hu - mus,
In the grave we shall end our strife,

Nos ha - be - bit hu - mus.
In the grave we shall end our strife.

Germany
MUß I DENN, MUß I DENN
(Must I Then, Must I Then)
Swabian Folksong, 1825

Muß i denn, muß i denn zum Städ-te-le hin-aus,
komm, wenn i komm, wenn i wie-der, wie-der komm,

Must I then, must I then to the cit-y go a-way,
turn, I'll re-turn, oh, yes, soon I will re-turn,

Städ-te-le hin-aus, und du, mein Schatz, bleibst
wie-der, wie-der komm, kehr i ein, mein Schatz, bei

must I got a-way, and you, my love, stay
and when I re-turn, I will stay with you, my

hier? Wenn i dir.   Kann i gleich nit all-weil
here? I'll re-dear.   Can I stay in-stead, re-

bei dir sei, han i doch mei Freud an
main with you, for you al-ways bring me

dir. Wenn i komm, wenn i komm, wenn i wierd'r-um komm,
cheer? I'll re-turn, I'll re-turn, oh, yes, here I'll re-turn,

wied'r-um komm, kehr i ein, mein Schatz, bei dir.
here I'll re-turn, and I'll stay with you, my dear.

Hungary

MAGASAN REPÜL A DARÙ
(Hungaria's Treasure)

1. Ma - ga-san re - pül a da-rù, szé - pen
2. Nin-csen ked-vem, mert a gól-ya el - vit
1. Lord, who gave to bright Hun-ga-ria grief and
2. Come, thou maid-en, find your peace in my em -

szól, Ha - rag-szik rám az én ró-zsám
te, Segy nagy ma - gas je - gen-ye-fá-
pain, looked at man, a hope-less crea-ture,
brace. Turn a-way those dark-ened clouds whose

mert, nem szól; Ne ha-ra-gudj é - des ba-bám!
ra tet - te; Ak-kor les-zek ked-ves róz-sám!
die in vain. Of-fered wine and love held by a
fears give chase. Let a kiss re-lease the pain in

so - ká - ig, Ti - éd va-gyok, ti - éd le-szek
a - ti - ed, Mi-kar az a, mi-kor az a
maid-en's heart. No-where else lies un-told beau-ty
which I dwell. For if ev-er dis-tance finds us,

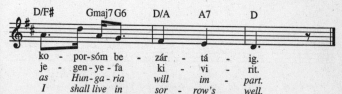

ko - por-sóm be - zár - tá - ig.
je - gen-ye-fa ki - vi - rit.
as Hun-ga-ria will im - part.
I shall live in sor - row's well.

Honduras
DORMITE NIÑITO
(Sleep, My Tiny Baby)

Dor – mi – te ni – ñi – to que ten – go que ha –
Sleep, my ti – ny ba – by; to work I must

cer, Lav – ar tus pañ – al – es,
go: I must wash your pant – ies,

sen – tar – me a co – ser. Dor – mi – te ni –
sit me down to sew. Sleep, my ti – ny

ñi – to, ca – be – za de ay – o – te,
ba – by, I prom – ise not to wake you.

Si no te dor – mis, te co – me el coy –
If you do not sleep, wolves will come and

89

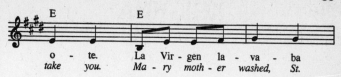

o – te. La Vir – gen la – va – ba
take you. Ma – ry moth – er washed, St.

Don Jo – se ten – dí – a, El Ni – ño llor –
Jos – eph spread the hay, While lit – tle ba – by

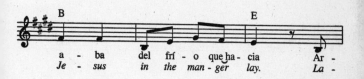

a – ba del frí – o que ha – cia Ar –
Je – sus in the man – ger lay. La –

ru, ar – ru – rú ar – ru, ar – ru –
loo, la – la – loo, la – loo, la – la –

rú, Ar – ru, ar – ru – rú, ar – ru –
loo, La loo, la – la – loo, la – la –

rú, ar – ru – rú.
loo, la – la – loo.

India

KRISHNA

"Krish - na, Krish - na, Kris - na" yen - du
"Krish - na, Krish - na, Krish - na" sing the

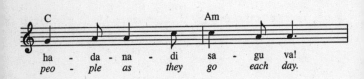

ha - da - na - di sa - gu va!
peo - ple as they go each day.

"Krish - na, Krish - na, Krish - na" yen - du
"Krish - na, Krish - na, Krish - na" let this

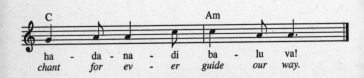

ha - da - na - di ba - lu va!
chant for ev - er guide our way.

Ireland
THE CROPPY BOY
Eighteenth Century

1. 'Twas ear - ly, ear - ly in the Spring, The
2. 'Twas ear - ly, ear - ly in the night, the
3. 'Twas in the guard-house where I was laid, and
4. As I was pass - ing my fa - ther's door, my
5. As I was go - ing up Wex - ford Hill, my
6. As I was moun - ted on the scaf - fold high, my
7. 'Twas in the Dun - gan - non this young man died, and

birds did whis - tle and sweet - ly sing, ___
yeo - man ca - val - ry gave me a fright.
in the par - lor where I was tried. ___
broth - er Wil - liam stood at the door.
who could blame me to cry my fill? ___
ag - ed fa - ther was stand - ing by. ___
in Dun - gan-non his bod - y lies. ___

Chang - ing their notes from tree to tree, ___ And the
The yeo - man ca - val - ry was my down - fall, and ___
My sen - tence passed and my cour - age low, ___ when to
My ag - ed fa - ther stood there al - so, ___ my ___
I looked be - hind and I looked be - fore, ___ my ___
My ag - ed fa - ther did me de - ny, ___ and the
And you good peo - ple that do pass by, ___ oh ___

song they sang ___ was "Old Ire - land Free."
ta - ken was I ___ by the Lord Corn - wall.
Dun - gan - non ___ I was forced to go.
ten - der moth - er her hair she tore.
ag - ed moth-er I shall see no more.
name he gave me was the Crop - py Boy.
shed a tear ___ for the Crop - py Boy.

Ireland

BENDEMEER'S STREAM

Words by Thomas Moore
Folk Melody

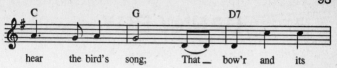

hear   the bird's   song;   That __ bow'r   and   its

mu - sic   I   ne'er   can   for - get,   But

oft   when a - lone   in the   bloom   of   the

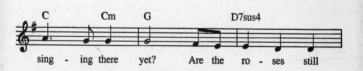

year,   I   think,   "Is   the   night - in - gale

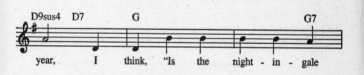

sing - ing there   yet?   Are the   ro - ses   still

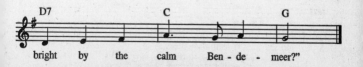

bright   by   the   calm   Ben - de - meer?"

Ireland
DANNY BOY
Words by Frederick Edward Weatherly
Folk Melody, "Londonderry Air"

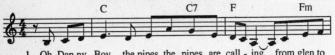

1. Oh, Dan-ny Boy, the pipes, the pipes are call - ing, from glen to
2. But if he come, when all the flow'rs are dy - ing, and I am

glen, and down the moun-tain side. The sum-mer's
dead, as dead I well may be, ye'll come and

gone, and all the ro - ses fall - ing, It's you, it's
find the place where I am ly - ing, and kneel and

you must go and I must bide. But come ye back when sum-mer's in the
say an A - ve there for me; And I shall hear, tho' soft your tread a -

mead - ow, or when the val - ley's hush'd and white with
bove me, and all my dreams will warm and sweet - er

snow. 'Tis I'll be there in sun-shine or in
be. If you will not fail to tell me that you

shad - ow, oh, Dan-ny Boy, oh Dan-ny Boy, I love you so!
love me, then I shall sleep in peace un-til you come to me!

Ireland

DOWN BY THE SALLEY GARDENS

Words by William Butler Yeats, 1889
Folk Melody

1. Down by the sal - ley gar - dens my love and I did meet. She passed the sal - ley gar - dens with lit - tle snow - white feet. She bid me take love eas - y, as the leaves grow on the tree. But I, be - ing young and fool - ish, with her did not a - gree.

2. In a field by the riv - er my love and I did stand. And lean - ing on my shoul - der she laid her snow - white hand. She bid me take life eas - y, as the grass grows on the weirs. But I was young and fool - ish, and now am full of tears.

Ireland
THE GALWAY PIPER

1. Ev - 'ry per - son in the na - tion
2. When the wed - ding bells are ring - ing,
3. When he walks the high - way peal - ing,

or of great or hum - ble sta - tion
his the breath that stirs the sing - ing.
'round his head the birds come wheel - ing.

holds in high - est es - ti - ma - tion,
Then in jigs the folks go swing - ing.
Tim has car - ols worth the steal - ing,

Pip - ing Tim of Gal - way.
What a splen - did pip - er!
Pip - ing Tim of Gal - way.

Loud-ly he can play, or low. He can move you, fast or slow.
He will blow from eve to morn, count-ing sleep a thing of scorn.
Thrush and lin - net, finch and lark to each oth - er twit-ter "Hark!"

Touch your hearts or stir your toe. Pip - ing Tim of Gal - way.
Old is he, but not out-worn. Know you such a pip - er?
Soon they sing from light to dark. Pip - ings learnt in Gal - way.

Ireland
GARRYOWEN

1. Let Bac - chus' sons be not dis-mayed, but
2. We are the boys that take de - light in
3. We'll break the win-dows, we'll break the doors, the
4. We'll beat the bail - iffs out of fun, we'll
5. Our hearts so stout have got us fame, for

join with me each jo - vi - al blade. Come
smash-ing the lime - rick lights when light - ing. Through
watch knock down by threes and fours. Then
make the may - ors and sher - iffs run. We
soon 'tis known from whence we came. Wher -

booze and sing and lend your aid, to
all the streets like sport - ers fight - ing, and
let the doc - tors work their cures, and
are the boys no man dares dun, if
e'er we go they dread the name of

help me with the cho - rus. }
tear - ing all be - fore us. }
tink - er up our brui - ses. } In -
he re - gards a whole skin. }
Gar - ry - o - wen in glo - ry.

stead of spa we'll drink down ale and pay the reck - 'ning

on the nail. No man for debt shall go to jail from

Gar - ry - o - wen in glo - ry.

Ireland
THE IRISH WASHERWOMAN

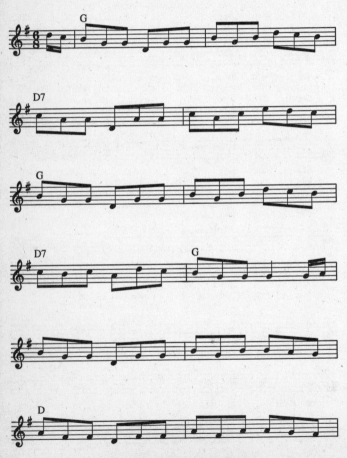

Ireland
KEVIN BARRY
Anonymous Words, Twentieth Century
English Folk Melody, "Rolling Home to Merry England"

1. In Mount-joy jail one Mon-day morn-ing, High up-on the gal-lows tree Kev-in Bar-ry gave his young life, For the cause of lib-er-ty, But a lad of eight-een sum-mers, Yet no one can de-ny As he walked to death that morn-ing, He proud-ly held his head on high.

2. Just be-fore he faced the hang-man, in his drear-y pri-son cell, Brit-ish sol-diers tor-tured Bar-ry just be-cause he would not tell. the names of his brave com-pan-ions and oth-er things they wished to know. "Turn in-form-er or we'll kill you," Ke-vin Bar-ry an-swered "No."

3. Calm-ly stand-ing to at-ten-tion, while he bade his last fare-well, to his bro-ken-heart-ed moth-er, whose grief no one can tell. For the cause he proud-ly cher-ished, this sad part-ing had to be. Then to death walked soft-ly smil-ing, that old Ire-land might be free.

4. An-oth-er Kevin mar-tyr for old Ire-land a-noth-er mur-der for the crown, whose bru-tal laws may kill the I-rish, but can't keep their spi-rit down. Lads like Bar-ry are no cow-ards, from the foe they will not fly. Lads like Bar-ry will free Ire-land, for her sake they'll live and die.

Ireland

THE LARK IN THE CLEAR AIR

Words and Music by Sir Samuel Ferguson, c. 1850

1. Dear thoughts are in my mind, and my
2. I shall tell her all my love, all my

soul soars en-chant-ed As I hear the sweet lark
soul's ad-o-ra-tion, And I think she will hear

sing in the clear air of the day. For a
me, and will not say me nay. It is

ten-der, beam-ing smile to my
this that gives my soul all its

hope has been grant-ed, And to-mor-row she shall
joy-ous e-la-tion, As I hear the sweet lark

hear all my fond heart would say.
sing in the clear air of the day.

Ireland

KITTY OF COLERAINE

1. As beau-ti-ful Kit-ty one morn-ing was trip-ping with a pitch-er of milk from the fair of Cole-raine: When she saw me, she stum-bled. The pitch-er, it tum-bled, and all the sweet but-ter-milk

2. I sat down be-side her and gen-tly did chide her that such a mis-for-tune should give her such pain. A kiss then I gave her, and be-fore I did leave her she vowed for such pleas-ure she'd

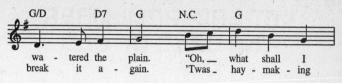

wa - tered the plain. "Oh, __ what shall I
break it a - gain. 'Twas __ hay - mak - ing

do now? 'Twas look - ing at you, now! Sure,
sea - son. I can't tell the rea - son. Mis -

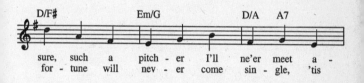

sure, such a pitch - er I'll ne'er meet a -
for - tune will nev - er come sin - gle, 'tis

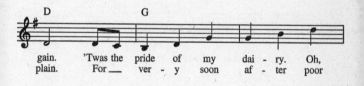

gain. 'Twas the pride of my dai - ry. Oh,
plain. For __ ver - y soon af - ter poor

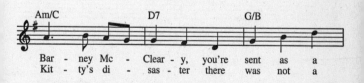

Bar - ney Mc - Clear - y, you're sent as a
Kit - ty's di - sas - ter there was not a

plague to the girls of Cole - raine!"
pitch - er found whole in Cole - raine!

Ireland

LET ERIN REMEMBER
THE DAYS OF OLD

Words by Thomas Moore
Folk Melody, "The Red Fox"

1. Let E - rin re - mem - ber the days of old, Ere her faith - less sons be - tray'd her; When Ma - lach - i wore the ____ col - lar of gold, Which he
2. On Lough Ne - agh's bank as the fish - er - man strays, Ere when her the clear, cold eve's de - clin - ing, he sees the round tow - ers of oth - er days, in the

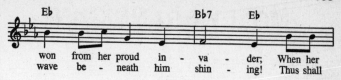

won from her proud in-va-der; When her
wave be-neath him shin-ing! Thus shall

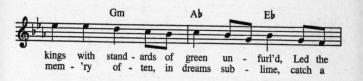

kings with stand-ards of green un-furl'd, Led the
mem-'ry of-ten, in dreams sub-lime, catch a

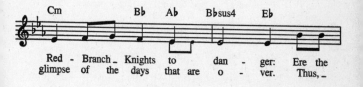

Red-Branch Knights to dan-ger: Ere the
glimpse of the days that are o-ver. Thus,

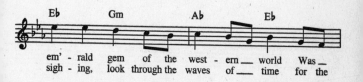

em'-rald gem of the west-ern world Was
sigh-ing, look through the waves of time for the

set in the crown of a stran-ger.
long fad-ed glo-ries they cov-er!

Ireland
MOLLY BRANNIGAN

1. Ma'am dear, did ye nev-er hear of
2. Ma'am dear, I re-mem-ber when the
3. The left side of my car-cass is as

pret-ty Mol-ly Bran-ni-gan____ In
milk-ing time was past and gone.____ We
weak as wa-ter gru-el, ma'am. There's

throth,____ then, she's left me and I'll
strolled____ thro' the mead-ow, and she
not a pick up-on my bones, since

nev-er be a man a-gain,
swore I was the on-ly one____
Mol-ly's proved so cru-el ma'am.

Not a spot on my hide will a
that ev-er she could love, but____
Oh, if I had a blun-der gun, I'd

sum-mer's sun e'er tan a-gain,____ since
oh, the base and cru-el one.____ For
go and fight a du-el, ma'am.____ For

Mol-ly's gone and left me here a-
all____ that she's left me here a-
sure I'd bet-ter shoot my-self than

Ireland
MOLLY MALONE
(Cockles and Mussels)

1. In Dub-lin's fair cit - y, where girls are so pret-ty, I first set my eyes on sweet Mol-ly Ma-lone. As she pushed her wheel - bar-row thro' streets broad and nar-row cry-ing "Cock-les and mus-sels, a - live, a - live, oh!
2. She was a fish - mon-ger, but sure 'twas no won-der, for so were her fa - ther and moth-er be-fore. And they each wheeled their bar-row thro' streets broad and nar-row cry-ing "Cock-les and mus-sels, a - live, a - live, oh!
3. She died of a fe - ver, and no one could save her, and that was the end of sweet Mol-ly Ma-lone. But her ghost wheels her bar-row thro' streets broad and nar-row cry-ing "Cock-les and mus-sels, a - live, a - live, oh!

A - live, a - live, oh! _ A - live, a - live, oh!" Cry-ing "cock-les and mus-sels, a - live, a - live, oh!"

Ireland
'TIS THE LAST ROSE
OF SUMMER
Words by Thomas Moore
Melody by Richard Alfred Milliken, "The Groves of Blarney"

1. 'Tis the last rose ___ of ___ sum-mer left ___
2. I'll ___ leave thee, ___ thou ___ lone one to ___
3. So ___ soon may I ___ fol-low, when ___

bloom - ing a - lone. All her love - ly ___ com -
pine ___ on a stem. Since the love - ly ___ are
friend - ships de - cay and from love's shin - ing

pan - ions are ___ fa - ded and ___ gone. No ___
sleep - ing, go ___ sleep thou with ___ them. Thus, ___
cir - cle the ___ gems ___ drop a - way. When ___

flow - er of her kin-dred, no ___ rose - bud is
kind - ly I ___ scat - ter thy ___ leaves ___ o'er the
true hearts lie ___ with-ered and ___ fond ___ ones are

nigh ___ to re - flect back ___ her ___ blush-es or ___
bed ___ where thy mates of ___ the ___ gar-den lie ___
flown, ___ oh, who would ___ in - hab - it this ___

give ___ sigh for sigh.
scent - less and ___ dead.
bleak ___ world a - lone?

Ireland
THE PARTING GLASS

1. O, _____ all the mon - ey _____
2. O, _____ all the com - rades _____
3. If _____ I had mon - ey e -

e'er I had, I _____ spent it in _____ good _____
e'er I had, they're _____ sor - ry for my go -
nough to spend, and _____ lei - sure time _____ to _____

com - pa - ny, And _____ all the harm I've _____
ing a - way. And _____ all the sweet - hearts _____
sit a - while, there _____ is a fair maid _____

ev - er done A - las! it was _____ to _____
e'er I had, they'd wish me one _____ more _____
in this town that _____ sore - ly has _____ my _____

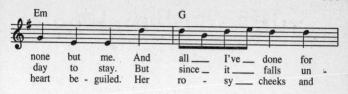

none but me. And   all __ I've __ done   for
day   to   stay. But   since __ it __ falls   un -
heart   be - guiled. Her   ro - sy __ cheeks   and

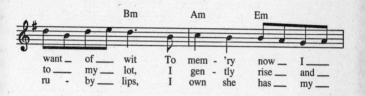

want __ of __ wit   To   mem - 'ry   now __ I __
to __ my __ lot,   I   gen - tly   rise __ and __
ru - by __ lips,   I   own   she   has __ my __

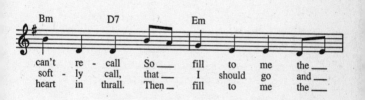

can't   re - call   So __ fill   to   me   the __
soft - ly   call,   that __ I   should   go   and __
heart   in   thrall. Then __ fill   to   me   the __

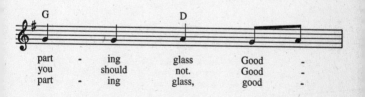

part - ing   glass   Good -
you   should   not.   Good -
part - ing   glass,   good -

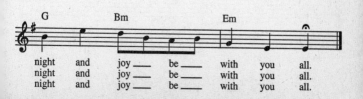

night   and   joy __ be __ with   you   all.
night   and   joy __ be __ with   you   all.
night   and   joy __ be __ with   you   all.

Ireland
THE WEARING OF
THE GREEN
Eighteenth Century

1. Oh __ Pad - dy dear, and did you hear the
2. Then __ since the col - or we must wear is
3. But, __ if at last our col - or should be

news that's go - ing 'round? The sham - rock is for -
Eng - land's cru - el red, sure Ire - land's sons will
torn from Ire - land's heart, her sons, with shame and

bid by law to grow on I - rish ground. Saint __
ne'er for - get the blood that they have shed. You may
sor - row, from the dear old soil will part. I've heard

Pat - rick's Day no more to keep. His col - or can't be
take the sham - rock from your hat and cast it on the
whis - pers of a coun - try that lies far be - yond the

seen, for there's a blood - y law a - gin' the
sod, but 'twill take root and flour - ish still, though
sea, where rich and poor stand e - qual in the

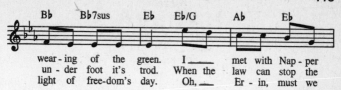

wear-ing of the green. I___ met with Nap-per
un-der foot it's trod. When the law can stop the
light of free-dom's day. Oh,___ Er-in, must we

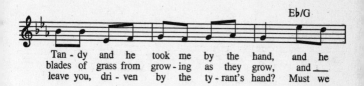

Tan-dy and he took me by the hand, and he
blades of grass from grow-ing as they grow, and___
leave you, dri-ven by the ty-rant's hand? Must we

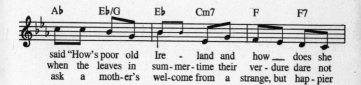

said "How's poor old Ire - land and how___ does she
when the leaves in sum-mer-time their ver-dure dare not
ask a moth-er's wel-come from a strange, but hap-pier

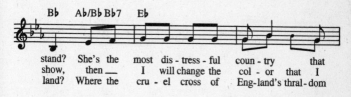

stand? She's the most dis-tress-ful coun-try that
show, then___ I will change the col-or that I
land? Where the cru-el cross of Eng-land's thral-dom

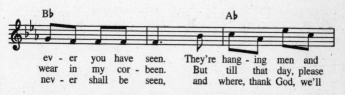

ev - er you have seen. They're hang - ing men and
wear in my cor - been. But till that day, please
nev - er shall be seen, and where, thank God, we'll

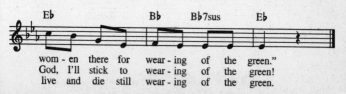

wom - en there for wear - ing of the green."
God, I'll stick to wear - ing of the green!
live and die still wear - ing of the green.

Israel
HATIKVA
Israeli National Anthem
Words by N.H. Imber
Folk Melody

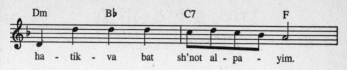

ha - tik - va bat sh'not al - pa - yim.

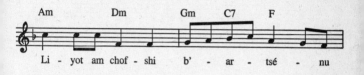

Li - yot am chof - shi b' - ar - tsé - nu

e - rets Tsi - yon Y' - ru - sha - la - yim.

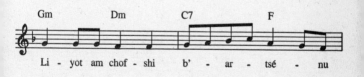

Li - yot am chof - shi b' - ar - tsé - nu

e - rets Tsi - yon Y' - ru - sha - la - yim.

Israel
HAVA NAGILA
Words by Moshe Nathanson
Music by Abraham Z. Idelsohn

Am

Ha - va n' - ra - n' na Ha - va n' - ra - n' na

B

Ha - va n' - ra - n' na v' - nis m' - cha

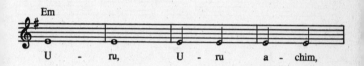

Em

U - ru, U - ru a - chim,

U - ru a - chim B' - lev sa - mey - ach, U - ru a - chim B' -

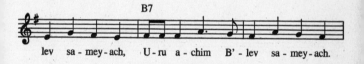

B7

lev sa - mey - ach, U - ru a - chim B' - lev sa - mey - ach.

U - ru a - chim B' - lev sa - mey - ach, U - ru a - chim,

Em

U - ru a - chim B'lev sa - mey - ach.

Israel

SHALOM CHAVEYRIM

(Shalom, My Friend)

Jewish Folksong

Sha - lom cha - vey - rim, sha -
Sha - lom, my___ friend, sha -

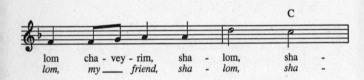

lom cha - vey - rim, sha - lom, sha -
lom, my___ friend, sha - lom, sha -

lom. L' - hit - ra - ot, l' -
lom. We'll meet a - gain, we'll

hit - ra - ot, sha - lom, sha - lom.
meet a - gain, sha - lom, sha - lom.

Israel
ZUM GALLI GALLI
Jewish Folksong

Zum Gal - li Gal - li Gal - li Zum Gal - li Gal - li

Zum Gal - li Gal - li Gal - li Zum Gal - li Gal - li.

He-cha-lutz le - man A - vo-dah A - vo-dah le -

man he-cha-lutz Ha-ba-chur le - man ba-chu-rah

Ba - chu - rah le - man ha - ba - chur.

Zum Gal - li Gal - li Gal - li Zum Gal - li Gal - li

Zum Gal-li Gal-li Gal-li Zum Gal-li Gal - li. Zum.

Israel

TUM BALALAIKA

Yiddish Folksong

E	E7	Am

ne - men, un nit far she - men.
beyn - ken, vey - nen on tre - ren.
wife for all of his life. _____
tears, al - though ___ it's yearn - ing?
tears, al - though ___ it's yearn - ing.

Am

Tum ba - la, tum ba - la, tum ba - la -

E7

lai - ka, Tum ba - la, tum ba - la,

Am   **F**

tum ba - la - lai - ka, tum ba - la - lai - ka,

G7   **C**   **Dm**

Shpil ba - la - lai - ka, Tum ba - la -
Play ba - la - lai - ka, Play ba - la -

E7   **Am**

lai - ka, Frey - lich zol zayn.
lai - ka, let there be joy.

Italy
LA VERA SORRENTINA
(The Fair Maid of Sorrento)
Naples

1. La ve - det - te a _____ Pie - di -
2. Dà chell' o - ra _____ nn'ag - gio
1. *Sweet your eyes at* _____ *Pie - di -*
2. *Peace for - ev - er* _____ *has de -*

grot - ta, tut - t'a fes - ta e - ra pa -
pa - ce, ston - go sem - pe a _____ sos - pe -
grot - ta *Filled my soul with* _____ *soft de -*
part - ed, *Night and day my* _____ *strength is*

ra - ta, pe guar - dà la _____ trup - pa
ra - re; cchiù la rez - za _____ non me
sir - ing, Trip - ping light - ly, _____ *by thy*
fail - ing, Then the rud - der _____ *help - less*

n'frot - ta, da la mam - ma ac - com - pa -
pia - ce, cchiù no nten - no _____ lo ppe -
moth - er. Pearls and gold was _____ *your at -*
leav - ing. To the great sea _____ *am I*

gna - ta. Na giac - chet - ta ag - gal - lo -
sca - re; Co la mi - se - ra var -
tir - ing. Laced with gold was _____ *all your*
sail - ing. Wretch - ed ves - sel, _____ *wild waves*

na - ta, na pet - ti - glia ___ ri - ca
chet - ta, A Sor - rien - to ___ nfret - ta
ves - ture, Silk - en ker - chief ___ shin - ing
leap - ing, Towards Sor - ren - to ___ swift - ly

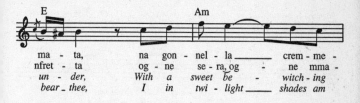

ma - ta, na gon - nel - la ___ crem - me
nfret - ta og - ne se - ra, og - ne mma -
un - der, With a sweet be - witch - ing
bear _ thee, I in twi - light ___ shades am

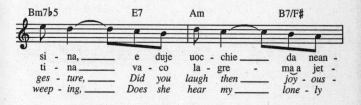

si - na, ___ e duje uoc - chie ___ da nean -
ti - na ___ va - co la - gre - ma a jet -
ges - ture, ___ Did you laugh then ___ joy - ous
weep - ing, ___ Does she hear my ___ lone - ly

tà, ___ E la bel - la ___ Sor - ren -
tà, ___ Ma la sgra - ta ___ Sor - ren -
ly, ___ Love - liest maid - en ___ of Sor -
cry? ___ Love - liest maid - en ___ of Sor -

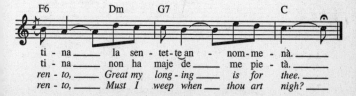

ti - na ___ la sen - tet - te an - nom - me - nà. ___
ti - na ___ non ha maje de ___ me pie - tà. ___
ren - to, ___ Great my long - ing ___ is for thee. ___
ren - to, ___ Must I weep when ___ thou art nigh? ___

Italy
SANTA LUCIA
Neapolitan Boat Song

1. Sul ma - re luc-ci-ca l'as - tro d'ar -
2. Con que - sto zef-fi - ro co - si so -
1. Now 'neath the sil - ver moon O - cean is
2. Here balm - y zeph-yrs blow, Pure joys in -

gen - to, pla - ci - da è l'on - da,
a - ve Oh! com' è bel - lo
glow - ing, O'er the calm bil - low
vite __ us, And as we gen - tly row

pros - pe - ro è il ven - to, sul ma - re
star sur la na - ve! con que - sto
Soft winds are blow - ing. Now 'neath the
All things de - light us. Here balm - y

luc-ci - ca l'as - tro d'ar-gen - to,
zef-fi - ro co - si so - a - ve
sil-ver moon O - cean is glow - ing,
zeph-yrs blow, Pure joys in - vite __ us,

pla - ci - da è l'on - da, pros - pe - ro è il
Oh! com' è bel - lo star sur la
O'er the calm bil - low Soft winds are
And as we gen - tly row All things de -

125

Italy
FI LA NANAE MI BEL FIOL
(Hushabye My Tiny Child)

Fi la na na e mi bel
Hush - a - bye my ti - ny

fiol, Fi la na na e mi bel
child, hush - a - bye, my ti - ny

fiol, Fa si la nan - na. _____
child and sleep till morn - ing. _____

Dor - mi ben, e mi bel
Sweet - ly sleep my ti - ny

fiol. Dor - mi ben, e mi bel
child, sweet - ly sleep my ti - ny

fiol, Fa si la nan - na.
child, oh sleep till morn - ing.

Jamaica

BANANA BOAT LOADER'S SONG

(Day Oh)

Work Song

Refrain

Day Oh Day_ Oh Day da light an' me

wan' go home. 1. Come Mis-ter Tall-y-man, Come tall-y me ba-na - na

Day da light an' me wan' go home. 2. Six hand, sev-en hand,
3. We load ba-na-nas till the
4. Some men work some

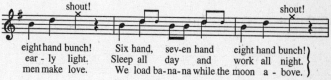

shout!
eight hand bunch! Six hand, sev-en hand eight hand bunch!
ear - ly light. Sleep all day and work all night.
men make love. We load ba-na-na while the moon a - bove.

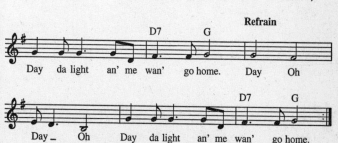

Refrain

Day da light an' me wan' go home. Day Oh

Day _ Oh Day da light an' me wan' go home.

Jamaica
HILL AND GULLY

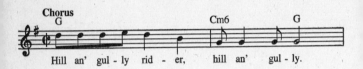

Hill an' gul-ly rid-er, hill an' gul-ly.

Hill an' gul-ly rid-er, hill an' gul-ly. I was

walk-in' real slow down hill an' gul-ly, when I

break my toe down hill an' gul-ly. Ma-ma

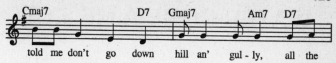

told me don't go down hill an' gul - ly, all the

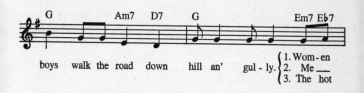

boys walk the road down hill an' gul - ly.

{
1. Wom-en
2. Me —
3. The hot
}

Verse

car-ry all the load down hill an' gul - ly, grass too
don-key like to run down hill an' gul - ly, I chase
sun — is a-burn-in' down hill an' gul - ly, I'm a-

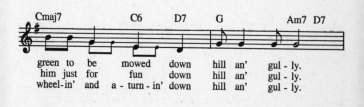

green to be mowed down hill an' gul - ly.
him just for fun down hill an' gul - ly.
wheel-in' and a-turn-in' down hill an' gul - ly.

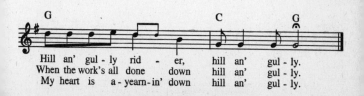

Hill an' gul - ly rid - er, hill an' gul - ly.
When the work's all done down hill an' gul - ly.
My heart is a-yearn-in' down hill an' gul - ly.

Jamaica
WATER COME A ME EYE

1. Ev - 'ry time I 'mem-ber Li - za, wa-ter come a me
2. I'm still wait-in' home for you __ wa-ter come a me
3. When there's love the time go fast __ wa-ter come a me
4. Lis - ten when you hear me call __ wa-ter come a me

eye. Ev - 'ry time I think 'pon Li - za,
eye. Heart is sore but wait - in' too __
eye. Time go slow when love is past __
eye. Please don't cause my heart to fall __

wa-ter come a me eye.
wa-ter come a me eye.
wa-ter come a me eye.
wa-ter come a me eye.

Come back, Li - za,

come back gal, wa - ter come a me eye.

Come back, Li - za, come back gal,

wa - ter comes a me eye.

Japan

KOMORIUTA
(Lullaby)

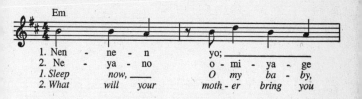

Em

1. Nen - ne - n yo; _____
2. Ne - ya - no o - mi - ya - ge
1. Sleep now, _____ O my ba - by,
2. What will your moth - er bring you

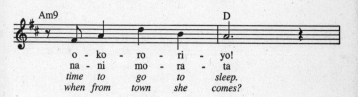

Am9   D

o - ko - ro - ri - yo!
na - ni mo - ra - ta
time to go to sleep.
when from town she comes?

Bo - ya - wa _____ yoi - ko - do
Den - den _____ tai - ko - ni
My _____ dear _____ dar - ling boy _____
Flutes _____ sweet _____ and _____ may - be

Am9   D   Em

nen - ne - shi - na.
she _____ ne - fu - e.
does - n't make a peep.
a great big bass drum.

Japan
SAKURA
(Cherry Blossoms)

Sa - ku - ra! Sa - ku - ra! Ya yo - i no
Sa - ku - ra! Sa - ku - ra! Cher - ry blos - soms

so ra __ wa Mi wa - ta - su
fill the __ air, Smell their fra - grance

ka - gi - ri Ka - su - mi ka
ev - 'ry - where. Win - ter - time is

ku - mo __ ka, Ni o - i - zo
fi - nally __ past, Now the spring is

i - zu - ru. I - za - ya! I - za - ya!
here at __ last. Come with me! Come with me!

Mi __ ni __ yu - kan.
Let us feel the sun - shine fair.

Latvia

AIJA, ANZIT, AIJA
(Lullaby)

1. Ai — ja, An — zit, ai — ja,
2. Augs tre — ja — das a — wis,
3. Tre — jeem sir — geem brau — za
1. *Lul — la — by my ba — by,*
2. *Ba — by lambs for ba — by,*
3. *We drove to your christ — 'ning*

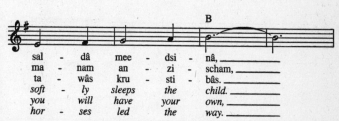

sal — dâ mee — dsi — nâ,
ma — nam an — zi — scham,
ta — wâs kru — sti — bâs.
soft — ly sleeps the child.
you will have your own,
hor — ses led the way.

Mah — sin te — wi schuh — pos,
Strupj — un ga — ra — sti — tes,
Deews dod an — zi — scha — mi
Sis — ter rocks you gen — tly,
you will be a ranch — er
You will drive such hor — ses

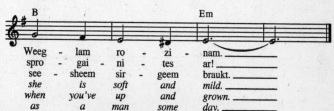

Weeg — lam ro — zi — nam.
spro — gai — ni — tes ar!
see — sheem sir — geem braukt.
she is soft and mild.
when you've up and grown.
as a man some day.

Kenya

SUKURU ITO
(When the Lion Coughs)

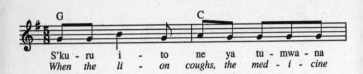

S'ku - ru   i - to   ne   ya   tu - mwa - na
When the li - on coughs, the med - i - cine

toi - ri - to,   A -   ru - ta - mi
men will dance, Jun - gle trees will

a -   yo   ne   ma - twen - de - te   mu - be
shake, for they fear his ter - ri - ble

no.   To -   ru   ta - guo   gu -
glance. The peo - ple all a -

tho -   ma   na   kwa - ndi - ka   kwa - ndi -
round will sac - ri - fice to soothe his

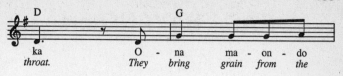

ka.   O - na   ma - on - do
throat.   *They bring grain from the*

mai - ngi ta go - ku - ru - ra mbi -
fields, fruit from trees, and man - y a

cha.   To - ho - ra - ga so -
goat.   *The li - on coughs, we*

rut   Tu - ka - ba - ra - ria
quake. *The moun - tains ech - o*

mo - go ta - to - kwe - nda ku - mbo - ka.____
back his might - y voice, and boul - ders break.____

Malaysia

RASA SAYANG EH
(Oh, to Be In Love)

Ra - sa sa - yang eh Ra - sa
Oh, to be in love! Oh, to

sa - yang sa - yang eh He - li - hat no - na
be in, be in love! I gaze up - on my

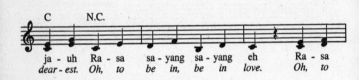

ja - uh Ra - sa sa - yang sa - yang eh Ra - sa
dear - est. Oh, to be in, be in love. Oh, to

sa - yang eh Ra - sa sa - yang sa - yang
be in love! Oh, to be in, be in

eh He - li - hat no - na ja - uh Ra - sa
love. I gaze up - on my dear - est. Oh, to

Fine **Verse**

sa - yang   sa - yang   eh.
be   in,   be   in   love.

{ 1. A - nak sem -
{ 2. Ka - lau a -
{ *1. Your eyes, they*
{ *2. My love for*

C

bi - lang di - ta - pak tan - gan   Pu - tik pa -
da su - mur di___ la - dang   Bo - leh sa -
spar - kle like beau - ti - ful jewels.   Your hair is
you is as deep as the sea.   My love for

uh de - li - ma ba - tu   Hi - lang di -
ya men - um - pang man - di   Ka - lau a -
gold   - en like the moon.   Your smile can
you is as pure as gold.   Oh, I will

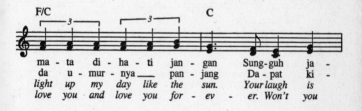

F/C   **C**

ma - ta di - ha - ti jan - gan   Sung - guh ja -
da u - mur - nya___ pan - jang   Da - pat ki -
light up my day like the sun.   Your laugh is
love you and love you for - ev - er.   Won't you

G7   **C**   **D.S. al Fine**

uh di - Neg - ri Sa - tu. }   Ra - sa
a ber - jum - pa la - gi. }
sweet mu - sic to my heart.}   Oh,   to
come spend your life with me? }

Mexico

CIELITO LINDO
(My Pretty Darling)

1. De la sie - rra mo - re - na, cie - li - to
2. U - na fle - cha en el ai - re, cie - li - to
3. To - das las ____ i - lu - sio - nes, cie - li - to
1. *From the Sie - rra Mo - re - na, my ____ pret - ty*
2. *Cu - pid let ____ fly an ar - row, my ____ pret - ty*
3. *All the air ____ y il - lu - sions, my ____ pret - ty*

lin - do, vie - nen ba - jan - do
lin - do, lan - zó Cu - pi - do
lin - do, que el ____ a - mor fra - gua,
dar - ling, there ____ came de - scend - ing ____
dar - ling, love's ____ fi - er - y dart. ____
dar - ling, that ____ love de - vis - es ____

un par de o - ji - tos ne - gros cie - li - to
y co - mo fué ____ ju - gan - do, cie - li - to
son com las ____ es - pu - mas, cie - li - to
one shin - ing pair ____ of dark eyes, my ____ pret - ty
And as he went a - way laugh - ing, my ____ pret - ty
are like the foam on the wa - ter, my ____ pret - ty

lin - do de ____ con - tra - ban - do. ____ }
lin - do, yo ____ fui el he - ri - do. ____ }
lin - do, que ____ for - ma el a - gua. ____ }
dar - ling, jewels ____ be - yond spend - ing. ____ }
dar - ling, it ____ struck my heart. ____ }
dar - ling, thin ____ as it ris - es. ____ }

iAy, ay, ay, ay! _____
iAy, ay, ay, ay! _____

Ay, ay, ay, ay! _____
Ay, ay, ay, ay! _____

can - ta y no llo - res, _____
su - ben y cre - cen _____

sing, don't be tear - ful, _____
surg - ing and grow - ing, _____

— por - que can - tan - do se a -
— y con el mis - mo _____

— be - cause a voice _____ that is
— and by the same _____ wind that

le - gran, cie - li - to lin - do, los _____
vien - to, cie - li - to lin - do, des -

sing - ing, my _____ pret - ty dar - ling, makes _
stirs them, my _____ pret - ty dar - ling, off _____

— co - ra - zo - nes. _____
- a - pa - re - cen. _____

— the heart cheer - ful. _____
they are blow - ing. _____

Mexico
FLOR, BLANCA FLOR
(Flower So White)

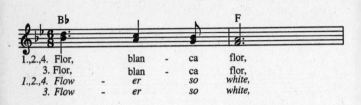

1.,2.,4. Flor, blan - ca flor,
3. Flor, blan - ca flor,
1.,2.,4. Flow - er so white,
3. Flow - er so white,

flor de las flo - res,_____ cha - pa -
flor de a - le lí - a, cha - pa -
bloom of per - fec - tion,_____ lit - tle
how you en - chant me, lit - tle

rri - ta de mi vi - da, re - gá -
rri - ta de mi vi - da,_____ re - gá -
sap - ling of my gar - den,_____ let me
sap - ling of my gar - den, hap - pi -

la - me tus a - mo - res._____ (1.En el
la - me tu a - le - grí - a. 2.En el
                                3.En el
bask in your af - fec - tion. 1.By the
ness I pray you grant me._____ 2.By the
*   3.By the*

141

mar ten-go u-na pal - ma___ con las
mar ten-go u-na pal - ma___ ver-de,
mar ten-go u-na pal - ma___ ver-de,
sea I have a palm tree, and its
sea I have a palm tree, green from
sea I have a palm tree, ver-dant

ra - mas has-ta el cie - lo___ don-de
ver - de has-ta la rá - iz; ___ yo te
ver - de has-ta el co - go - llo; ___ yo te
boughs touch con - stel - la - tions; there my
root to lit - tle knob - bies; I will
life its na - ture quick - ens; I will

se re - fu - gia mi al - ma___ cuan-do
si - go, mi chi - ni - ta, co - mo
si - go, mi chi - ni - ta, co - mo el
wea - ry soul finds ref - uge when it
fol - low you, my blos - som, as pig -
fol - low you, my blos - som, as the

no en - cuen - tra con - sue - lo.
los puer - cos al má - iz. ___
ga - vi - lán al
knows no con - so - la - tions. ___
gies chase the corn cob - bies. ___
hawk pur - sues the

D.C. al Fine

po - llo.

chick - ens. ___

Mexico
LA CUCARACHA
Mexican Revolution

1. Con las bar-bas de Ca-rran-za
1. With the whisk-ers of Ca-rran-za

voy a ha-cer u-na to-qui-lla
I shall weave a hand-some band___

pa po-ner-se-la al som-bre-ro
for the hat of Pan-cho Vi-lla;

de su pa-dre Pan-cho Vi-lla. La cu-ca-
he'll be fair-est in the land.___ La cu-ca-

ra-cha, la cu-ca-ra-cha
ra-cha, la cu-ca-ra-cha

ya no pue-de ca-mi-nar,___ por-que no
can-not jour-ney out to-day,___ be-cause he's

tie-ne, por-que le fal-ta
lack-ing, be-cause he has-n't

ma - ri - hua - na   que   fu - mar.
an - y   pot   to   ease   his   way.

2. Ya murió la cucaracha,
   ya la llevan a enterrar,
   entre cuatro zopilotes
   y un ratón de sacristán.
   (CHORUS)

2. *Now the cucaracha died,*
   and they took him from the house
   to be buried near four buzzards
   and a peaceable church mouse.
   (CHORUS)

3. Con las barbas de Forey
   voy a hacer un vaquerillo,
   pa ponérselo al caballo
   del valiente don Porfirio.
   (CHORUS)

3. *With the whiskers of old Forey*
   I shall make a doll, of course,
   to be set upon the saddle
   of Porfirio's noble horse.
   (CHORUS)

4. Para sarapes, Saltillo;
   Chihuahua, para soldados;
   para mujeres, Jalisco;
   para amar, toditos lados.
   (CHORUS)

4. *Who's for ponchos? It's Saltillo.*
   Chihuahua's the soldiers' choice.
   And for women, it's Jalisco.
   But for love, all raise one voice.
   (CHORUS)

5. Un panadero fué a misa,
   no encontrando qué rezar,
   le pidió a la Virgen pura
   marijuana que fumar.
   (CHORUS)

5. *Once a baker was at Mass,*
   but could not find words to pray,
   so he asked the Blessed Virgin
   for some pot to ease his way.
   (CHORUS)

6. Un zapatero fué a misa,
   no encontrando qué rezar,
   andaba por todas partes:
   —"Zapatos que remendar."—
   (CHORUS)

6. *Once a cobbler was at Mass,*
   but could not find words to pray,
   so he walked around the church:
   "I'll repair your shoes today."
   (CHORUS)

7. Una cosa me da risa;
   Pancho Villa sin camisa:
   ya se van los carrancistas,
   porque vienen los villistas.
   (CHORUS)

7. *One thing makes me laugh so loudly:*
   Pancho Villa with no shirt.
   Now the Carranzistas vacate;
   Villa's men could make them hurt.
   (CHORUS)

8. Necesito un automóvil
   para hacer la caminata
   al lugar donde mandó
   a la Convención Zapata.
   (CHORUS)

8. *I could really use a car now;*
   I must travel — did I mention?
   I must go where I've been ordered:
   to Zapata's big Convention.
   (CHORUS)

Morocco
ZOHRA
Kabyle Folksong

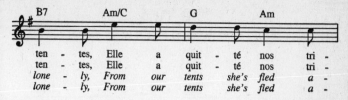

ten - tes, Elle a quit - té nos tri -
lone - ly, From our tents she's fled a

bus, En - vo - lez - vous, lu - eurs char -
way. Gone for - ev - er is love's bright en -

man - tes, Ma Zoh - ra Je ne la ver - rai
chant - ment, Zoh - ra, sweet, I shall nev - er see

plus. En - vo - lez - vous, pro - mes - ses en - i -
more, For vain her prom - is - es, vain my a -

vran - tes, Ma Zoh - ra Je ne la ver - rai plus.
dor - ing, Zoh - ra, sweet, I shall nev - er see more.

Lithuania
DAINA
(From Afar Returns My Dear Beloved)

Netherlands
HOE LAAT IS'T?
(What Time Is It?)

Hoe laat is't? twaalf hur. Wie
"The clock says it's twelve." *to*

is bij? de meid. Waar is zij? in de
an - swer the maid. Where is she? in the

keu - ken. Wat doet zij? zij breit. Voor
kitch - en. She sits and she knits. For

wie? Voor wie? Voor de klei - ne pop - pe -
who? For who? For the ba - by, lit - tle

dei - ne, En de groo - ten bim - bam.
ba - by, And the clock goes tick - tock.

Netherlands
ROSA
Flemish Dance Tune

1. Ro - sa, wil - len wy dan - sen? Danst
2. Ro - sa, wil - len wy min - nen? Mint,
3. Ro - sa, wil - len wy trou - wen? Trouwt
1. Ro - sa, dear, shall we dance, then? Dance,
2. Ro - sa, dear, shall we kiss then? Kiss,
3. Ro - sa, wilt thou be mine then? Dear

Ro - sa! danst Ro - sa! Ro - sa, wil - len wy
Ro - sa! mint Ro - sa! Ro - sa, wil - len wy
Ro - sa! trouwt Ro - sa! Ro - sa, wil - len wy
Ro - sa! dance, Ro - sa! Ro - sa, dear, shall we
Ro - sa! kiss Ro - sa! Ro - sa, dear, shall we
Ro - sa! dear Ro - sa! Ro - sa, wilt thou be

dan - sen? Danst Ro - sa zoet! _____
min - nen? Mint Ro - sa zoet! _____
trou - wen? Trowt Ro - sa zoet! _____
dance then? Dance, Ro - sa sweet! _____
kiss then? Kiss, Ro - sa sweet! _____
mine then? Dear Ro - sa sweet! _____

Ro - sa med hear bloe - men - hoed _____
Ro - sa med hear bloe - men - hoed _____
Ro - sa med hear bloe - men - hoed _____
Ro - sa with her hat of flow - ers
Ro - sa with her hat of flow - ers
Ro - sa with her hat of flow - ers

Zy had-de geld, maer wei-nig good, danst Ro - sa
Zy had-de geld, maer wei-nig good, danst Ro - sa
Zy had-de geld, maer wei-nig good, danst Ro - sa
Ah! nei-ther wealth nor lands has she, But danc - es
Ah! nei-ther wealth nor lands has she, But kiss - es
Ah! nei-ther wealth nor lands has she, Wilt thou be

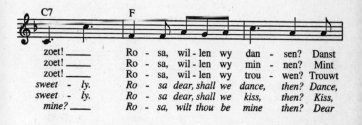

zoet! ____ Ro - sa, wil-len wy dan - sen? Danst
zoet! ____ Ro - sa, wil-len wy min - nen? Mint
zoet! ____ Ro - sa, wil-len wy trou - wen? Trouwt
sweet - ly. *Ro - sa dear, shall we dance, then? Dance,*
sweet - ly. *Ro - sa dear, shall we kiss, then? Kiss,*
mine? ____ *Ro - sa, wilt thou be mine then? Dear*

Ro - sa! danst Ro - sa, Ro - sa, wil-len wy
Ro - sa! mint Ro - sa! Ro - sa, wil-len wy
Ro - sa! trouwt Ro - sa! Ro - sa, wil-len wy
Ro - sa, dance, Ro - sa! *Ro - sa, dear, shall we*
Ro - sa, kiss Ro - sa! *Ro - sa, dear, shall we*
Ro - sa, dear Ro - sa! *Ro - sa, wilt thou be*

dan - sen? Danst Ro - sa zoet! ____
min - nen? Mint Ro - sa zoet! ____
trou - wen? Trouwt Ro - sa zoet! ____
dance then? Dance, Ro - sa *sweet! ____*
kiss then? Kiss, Ro - sa *sweet! ____*
mine then? Dear Ro - sa *sweet! ____*

Netherlands
WAER DAT MEN SICH
(Where'er Man Ranges)
Battle Song, 1616

1. Waer dat men sich al keerd of wend, end waer men loopt of staet, Waer dat men reijst of rotst of rend, end waer men he - nen gaet, Daer
2. Ver - een - igt vrij ge - voch - ten volk maeckt Span - jen d'oor log moe. Sulcx dot hij zij - nen vre - den - tolck dit land moet sen - den toe. Wie
3. O Neer - land! So ghij maer en bout op God den Heer al - tijdt. U - pij - len vast ge - bon - den hout, saem een - drach - tig zijt. So

1. Wher - e'er man rang - es 'neath the sun, Wher - e'er he goes or stays; What ev - er dis - tant course may run, Up on the earth's wide ways, The
2. A brave, u - nit - ed war - like land, we fought the Span - iards long. win - ning peace on ev - 'ry hand, gen - tle, true, and strong. We
3. O Neth - er - lands, on God re - ly, if stead - fast thou wouldst stand. With faith un - shak - en, hon - or high, a brave, a ho - ly land. Then

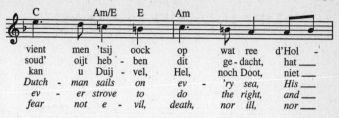

vient	men	'tsij	oock	op	wat	ree	d'Hol -
soud'	oijt	heb -	ben	dit	ge -	dacht,	hat
kan	u	Duij -	vel,	Hel,	noch	Doot,	niet
Dutch -	*man*	*sails*	*on*	*ev -*	*'ry*	*sea,*	*His*
ev -	*er*	*strove*	*to*	*do*	*the*	*right,*	*and*
fear	*not*	*e -*	*vil,*	*death,*	*nor*	*ill,*	*nor*

lan -	der	end	de	Zeeuw:	Sij
d'hoog -	moet	van	Pa -	pou.	Dat
kren -	cken	noch	ver -	treen.	Al
com -	*rade*	*by*	*his*	*side,*	*And*
thus	*a*	*king -*	*ly*	*foe*	*laid*
all	*the*	*pow'r*	*of*	*Spain.*	*Thy*

loo -	pen	door	de	woes -	te	Zee,	als
soo	een	groo -	te	trot -	se	macht	so
waer	oock	Span -	jen	noch	so	groot,	ja
li -	*on -*	*heart -*	*ed,*	*proud,*	*and*	*free,*	*They*
down	*his*	*arms*	*be -*	*fore*	*our*	*might,*	*his*
God	*thy*	*stength*	*will*	*'stab -*	*lish*	*still,*	*Thy*

door	het	bosch	de	Leeuw.
buij -	gsaem	wor -	den	sou?
s'wer -	elts	mach -	ten	een.
breast	*the*	*foam -*	*ing*	*tide.*
haught -	*y*	*head*	*bent*	*low.*
free -	*dom*	*will*	*main -*	*tain.*

Nigeria

I WILL FEED MY BABY

Yoruba Lullaby

I will cook some food for my — lit-tle ba-by, — I — will feed my ba-by, oh my lit-tle child. And my child will feed me when I'm — old and tired. Yes — my child will care for me when I'm in need. Like the sheep that feeds its lamb, I'll feed my child. Like the sheep that feeds its lamb, I'll feed my child. I will cook some food for my — lit-tle ba-by, — I — will feed my ba-by, oh my lit-tle child.

Norway

NAA SKA'EN LITEN FAA SOVA SOA SÖDT
(Here Is the Cradle)

Naa ska'en li-ten faa so-va soa södt,
Here is the cra-dle pre-pared for your sleep,

Vög-ga staar re-je te baa-ne,
Safe and so warm, lit-tle ba-by.

Der ska' en lig-ge saa vart aa saa blödt,
An-gels shall come soon, their vig-il to keep,

Trygt-kan de so-va de baa-ne,
Watch o-ver you lit-tle ba-by.

Ro Ro so-va saa södt, Guds
Loo loo, now go to sleep, So

en-gel tar va-re paa baa-ne.
sweet-ly to sleep, lit-tle ba-by.

Norway

HJEMREISE FRA SAETEREN
(Homeward from the Mountains)
Shepherd's Song

1. Os ha gjort, kva gje - ras skul - le,
2. Far - vael kve, som of - te gjo - re
3. Far - vael Mork, som Fae - nan gnaa - gaa,
1. To the val - ley comes the herds - man,
2. Fare ye well, o dew - y mead - ows,
3. Here on high, wild winds will wan - der,

y - sta Ost aa kjin - na Smör,
blau - fast Blom - ster - seng pum me,
der e gjaet - te man - gein Gaang.
to his hearth and home so dear,
shad - owed woods, and moun - tains one
swift - ly home - ward let us go,

Naa staa att aa klöv - ja Öy - kjom
naer e trott ve Hog - sdags Loy - te
Far - vael skog, som of - te jo - ma
Rich - ly la - den, for his la - bor
whence a far oft sent I greet - ing,
where sweet love waits in the vil - lage,

set - ja Laar for Sae - ter - dör.
jö paa slong - de me paa de.
taa min Lur aa Stut aa Saang!
is all fin - ished for the year.
with my horn's clear sil - v'ry tone.
twink - ling lights of wel - come glow.

Bb F C7

Kork - je fins ___ dae mei - re Fö - e
Far - vael Sael, ___ mi kjae - re stu - gu
Far - vael Hul - der, som daer bud - de!
Safe - ly guard - ed is his cot - tage
Fare ye well, ___ kind - heart - ed hill - folk,
Joy - ous shall ___ we greet our dear ones,

Am Dm G7 C7

haer for Hei - e hell for Krist;
Som saa mangt ___ mitt Ar - bei saag.
flot naa du - 'ti sae - le inn.
from wild win - ter's storm and rain,
dwell - ing on these pine - clad heights,
wealth we bear ___ for win - ter's store.

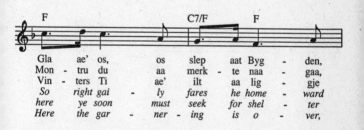

F C7/F F

Gla ae' os, os slep aat Byg - den,
Mon - tru du aa merk - te naa - gaa,
Vin - ters Ti ae' ilt aa lig - gje
So right gai - ly fares he home - ward
here ye soon must seek for shel - ter
Here the gar - ner - ing is o - ver,

C7/F F

mei - re gla ae' Ku - e vist.
naer Sta - kal - lens jaa meg laag?
u - te baa for Vaer aa Vind.
to the vil - lage once a - gain.
from the storm - y win - ter nights.
lone - ly heights, fare - well once more.

Norway

JEG LAGDE MIG SAA SILDE
(I Laid Me Down to Rest)

1. Jeg lag - de mig saa sil - de 'og
2. Saa gan - ger jeg mig op i
3. Saa gik jeg jeg mig ud paa

1. I laid me down to rest, and the
2. Then quick - ly I sped to her
3. I fled from the room to the

seent om en Kveld, Jeg
Hpi - en loft, Som
gron - nen Eng, Der

hour it was late, I
home in the hills, where
mead - ow green, the

vid - ste af slet in - gen
jeg ple - ied van til at
hor - te jeg de Klok - ker

knew nought of pain or ach - ing
of - ten I wished to be
bells in the church - tower were

Kvi - de; Da kom der et
gjo - re. Der Ik - ke stan - der de
rin - ge. Then word came to

sor - row; Then word came to
far - ing. A group of fair
toll - ing. But noth - ing I

157

Bm/D · G7 · Bm · F#m/A

Bud i fra Kjae - re - sten
Jom - fruer alt u - di
vid - ste ik - ke An - det jeg for -
me from my sweet - heart so
maid - ens sur - round - ed my
heard, nought but an - guish did I

D · G · D

min, Jeg skul - de til
Flok og Klae - de til min
nam, End mit Hjer - te i
dear To her has - ten to
love, her form for the
know, my heart's grief was

Em7 · D/F# · G6b5 · F# · **Chorus** Bm · Em

hen - de bort - ri - de. ⎫
Kjar - est til Do - de. ⎬
Styk - ker mon sprin - ge. ⎭ Tvun - get ha - ver
her ere the mor - row. ⎫
cold grave pre - par - ing. ⎬ *No one have I*
far past con - sol - ing. ⎭

Bm/F# · F# · Bm

El - sko - ven hen - de.
ev - er loved so dear - ly.

Poland
KRAKOWIAK
(Darling Maiden, Hark, I Ask Thee)

1. U - klad ze mna zrób, dzie - wecz - ko, zo - czy - wi - stym
2. Dzié - wcze sie na to u - smié - cha nic nie mó - wi,
1. *Dar - ling maid - en, hark, I ask thee. I would like to*
2. *Light - ly laughs the pret - ty wom - an. From her red lips*

two - im zys - kiem jac dam piosn - ke za pios - necz - ka
wiec ze - zwa - la; ja zac - zy - nam spie - wac zci - cha
make a bar - gain. I'll sing you some love___ songs if
comes no an - swer. With my pas - sion - lad - en sing - ing,

ty mi u - ścisk___ za u - ścis - kiem.
tra la la___ la,___ tra la___ la la.
you will kiss___ me___ sweet - ly and gen - tly.
I will cap - ture the heart of this wom - an.

Przy u - kla - dzie tym ob - sta - waj a___ wa - ru - jac
Spié - wam cia - gle, o - na slu - cha sa - dze___ wiec___ o
Nev - er was there such a fine trade, songs___ of___ pas - sion for
I will sing till her eyes dark - en, filled___ with___ love___ and

so - bie zy - ski ty mi pio - snek nie od - da - waj
téj fi - lu - tce Ze gdy mi na - dsta - wia u - cha
man - y kiss - es. Can I claim my songs a - gain and
sweet af - fec - tion. So that we may share these pleas - ures,

ja___ ci___ od - dam___ twe u - sci - ski.
od - da___ mi i___ ser - ce w kro - tce.
sing___ them___ for more kiss - es from my sweet maid?
please,___ I___ ask thee, maid - en, hark - en.___

Portugal

MODINHA
(Why Do You Your Lips Deny Me?)

Por - que me di - zes cho - ran - do,
Why do you your lips de - ny me?

Que te não lem - bras de mim,
Hate will nev - er hold your heart.

Se teos ays, se teos su - spi - ros
Let me lin - ger but be - side thee,

E - stão me di - zen - do que sim.
your eyes say we'll nev - er part.

Se teos ays, se teos su - pi - ros
Let me lin - ger but be - side _____ thee,

E - stão me di - zen - do que sim.
Your eyes say we'll nev - er part.

Russia
DUBINUSHKA
(Sledgehammer Song)

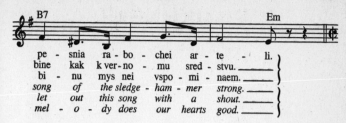

pe - snia ra - bo - chei ar - te - li.
bine kak k ver - no - mu sred - stvu. ____
bi - nu mys nei vspo - mi - naem. ____
song of the sledge - ham - mer strong. ____
let out this song with a shout. ____
mel - o - dy does our hearts good. ____

Refrain
Twice as fast

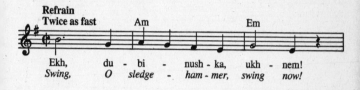

Ekh, du - bi - nush - ka, ukh - nem!
Swing, O sledge - ham - mer, swing now!

Ekh, ze - lë - na - ia sa -
Put your back in - to it, ____

ma poi - dët! Po - dër - nem, po -
there you go. And one now, and

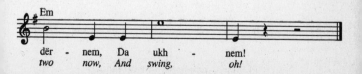

dër - nem, Da ukh - nem!
two now, And swing, oh!

Russia

EI, UKHNEM!
(Song of the Volga Boatmen)
Work Song

Refrain

Ei, ___ ukh - nem! Ei, ___ ukh - nem!
Yo, ___ heave ho! *Yo, ___ heave ho!*

E - shchë raz - ik e - shchë raz!
Stea - dy, ea - sy, once ___ a - gain!

Verse

1. Raz - o - v'ëm ___ my ___ be - rë - zu,
2. My po be - rezh - ku i - dëm,
3. Ekh, ty, Vol - ga, ___ mat' - re - ka,

1. *Strike the birch ___ tree ___ tow - 'ring high,*
2. *Float - ing down ___ the ___ stream we sing,*
3. *Vol - ga it ___ de - serves our praise,*

Raz - o - v'ëm ___ my ___ ku - dria - vu,
pes - niu sol - nysh - ku po - ëm.
shi - ro - ka i ___ glu - bo - ka.
keep the pace ___ un - til you die.
gold - en light ___ the ___ sun will bring.
flow - ing strong ___ in ___ all its ways.

Ai da, da, ai da, Ai da, da, ai da,
Ay - da, da, ay - da! Ay - da, da, ay - da!

Raz - o - v'ëm __ my ku - dria - vu.
Pes - niu sol - nysh - ku __ po - ëm
Shi - ro - ka __ i glu - bo - ka.
Strike the birch __ tree tow - 'ring high.
Float - ing down __ the stream __ we sing.
Flow - ing strong __ in all __ its ways.

1.
Ei, __ ukh - nem!
Yo, __ heave ho!

2.
Ei, __ ukh - nem!
Yo, __ heave ho!

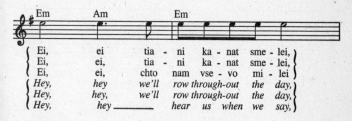

Ei, ei tia - ni ka - nat sme - lei,
Ei, ei, tia - ni ka - nat sme - lei,
Ei, ei, chto nam vse - vo mi - lei
Hey, hey we'll row through-out the day,
Hey, hey we'll row through-out the day,
Hey, hey __ hear us when we say,

Pes - niu sol - nysh - ku __ po - ëm.
Pes - niu sol - nysh - ku __ po - ëm.
Vol - ga, Vol - ga, __ mat' - re - ka.
sing - ing to the __ warm-ing light __ a - bove.
sing - ing to the __ warm-ing light __ a - bove.
Vol - ga, Vol - ga __ it de - serves __ our praise.

Russia
KALINKA
(Little Snowball Bush)

Chorus

Ka - lin - ka, ka - lin - ka, ka - lin - ka ma - ia! V sa - du ia - go - da ma - lin - ka, ma - lin - ka mo - ia. Ka - ia. Akh, _____

Ka - lin - ka, ka - lin - ka, ka - lin - ka of mine! In the ar - bor grows a ber - ry as sweet as red wine. Ka - wine. Oh, _____

1. pod _____ sos - no - nush - iv,
2. so - së _____ nush - ka,
3. kra - sa - vit - sa,

1. un - der the _____ oak tree,
2. lit - tle _____ oak tree,
3. oh, my dear _____ maid - en,

Russia

VO POLE BERËZYN'KA
STOIALA
(In the Forest Grew a Tiny Birch Tree)

1. Vo po - le be - rë - zyn'- ka sto - ia - la.
2. Ne - ko - mu be - rë - zu za - lo - ma - ti.
3. Poi - du ia v les___ po - gul - ia - iu,
1. In the for - est grew a ti - ny birch___ tree.
2. No one ev - er harmed the ti - ny birch___ tree.
3. To the for - est now, with hatch - et swing - ing;

Vo po - le kud - ria - va - ia sto - ia - la.
Ne - ko - mu kud - ria - vu zash - chi - pa - ti.
be - lu - iu be - rë - zu za - lo - ma - iu.
In the for - est grew a ten - der birch___ tree.
No one dared to chop the ten - der birch___ tree.
all to end the sil - ver birch tree's grow - ing.

Liu - li, liu - li li sto - ia - la,
Liu - li, liu - li, za - lo - ma - ti;
Liu - li, liu - li, po - gul - ia - iu;
La la, la la, a birch tree;
La la, la la, the birch tree;
La la, la la, swing - ing;

Chorus

Liu - li, liu - li sto - ia - la.
liu - li liu - li zash - chi - pa - ti. }
liu - li liu - li za - lo - ma - iu.
La la, la la, a birch tree.
la la, la la, the birch tree. }
la la, la la sing - ing.

Ta - ry,

Then the

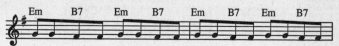

bary, ras-ta-bary, Sne-gi be-ly vy-pa-da-li, Se-ry
snow-flakes down-ward glid-ing Gave the rab-bits mea-ger hid-ing As the

zai-tsy vy-be-ga-li, O-khot-ni-ki vy-ez-zha-li, Vsekh so-
grey-hounds barked their guid-ing To the hunt-ers, hors-es rid-ing. Then they

bak svo-ikh spu-ska-li, Kras-nu dev-ku is-pu-ga-li.
home, to wife a-bid-ing, Has-en-pfef-fer* were pro-vid-ing.

Ty, de-vi-tsa, stoi, stoi, stoi, stoi! Kra-sa-vi-tsa s na-mi pes-niu
Let us sing a song, sing, sing, sing! Let us sing and let the bells go

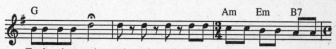

poi, poi, poi! Chu-vil', moi chu-vil', chu-vil',
ding dong ding! Fa la, fa la la, fa la,

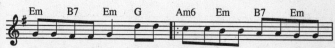

Na-vil', vil', vil', vil'. E-shchë chu-do, per-vo chu-do, Chu-do
La la, la, la, la. It's the truth that I am tell-ing, Oh, yes

ro-di-na mo-ia. E-shchë ro-di-na mo-ia.
ev-'ry word is true. It's the ev-'ry word is true.

* "Hasenpfeffer" is rabbit stew.

Russia
TROIKA MCHITSIA
(Troika Rushing)
Words by P. Vyazemsky
Music by P. Bulakhov

Refrain:

* "Troika" is a Russian vehicle driven by a team of horses.

Scotland
BALOO BALEERIE

Refrain

Ba - loo ba - lee - rie, ba -
loo ba - lee - rie, ba - loo ba -
lee - rie, Ba - loo ba - lee.

Verse

Gang a -
Down —
Sleep —

wa' pee - rie fair - ies, gang a - wa' pee - rie
come the bon - ny an - gels, down — come the bon - ny
saft my — ba - by, sleep — saft my —

fair - ies. Gang a - wa' pee - rie
an - gels. Down — come the bon - ny
ba - by. Sleep — saft my —

fair - ies. Frae oor ben noo.
an - gels. Tae oor ben noo.
ba - by. In oor ben noo.

Scotland
BARBARA ALLEN

Expressively

1. In Scar - let Town, where I was born; There
2. 'Twas in the mer - ry month of May, When
3. He sent a ser - vant to the town, The
4. And as she crossed the wood - ed fields, She
5. O Moth - er, Moth - er, make my bed, And
6. "Fare - well," she said, "ye maid - ens all, And

was a fair maid dwell - in', Made
green buds they were swell - in'. Sweet
place where she was dwell - in'. "My
heard his death - bell knell - in', And
make it long and nar - row. Sweet
shun the fault I fell in: Hence -

ev - 'ry youth cry ____ Well - a - day! Her
Wil - liam on his ____ death - bed lay For
mas - ter's sick and ____ bids you come If
ev - 'ry stroke, it ____ spoke her name, "Hard -
Wil - liam died for ____ love of me; I'll
forth take warn - ing ____ by the fall Of

name was Bar - b'ra Al - len.
love of Bar - b'ra Al - len.
you be Bar - b'ra Al - len."
heart - ed Bar - b'ra Al - len."
die for him of sor - row."
cru - el Bar - b'ra Al - len.

Scotland

THE BLUE BELLS
OF SCOTLAND

Attributed to a Mrs. Jordon, c. 1800

1. Oh where, tell me where is your __ High-land lad-die gone? Oh where, tell me where is your __ High-land lad-die gone? He's gone wi' stream-ing ban - ners where __ no-ble deeds are done, And it's oh, in my heart I __ wish him safe at home.

2. Oh where, tell me where did your __ High-land lad-die dwell? Oh where, tell me where did your __ High-land lad-die dwell? He dwelt in bon-nie Scot - land, where __ blooms the sweet blue bell. And it's oh, in my heart I __ lo'e my lad-die well.

3. Oh what, tell me what does your __ High-land lad-die wear? Oh what, tell me what does your __ High-land lad-die wear? A bon - net with a lof - ly plume, and __ on his breast a plaid. And it's oh, in my heart I __ lo'e my High-land lad.

4. Oh what, tell me what if your __ High-land lad be slain? Oh what, tell me what if your __ High-land lad be slain? Oh, no, true love will be his guard and __ bring him safe a - gain. For it's oh, my heart would break if my __ High-land lad were slain.

Scotland
CHARLIE IS MY DARLING
Words variously attributed to James Hogg or Lady Carolina Nairne
Folk Melody

Oh! Char-lie is my dar-ling, my dar-ling my dar-ling! Oh!

Char-lie is my dar-ling, the young che-va-lier.

1. 'Twas
2. As
3. Wi'
4. They've
5. Oh!

on a Mon-day morn - ing, Right ear-ly in the year, When
he cam' march-in' up the street, The pipes played loud and clear; And
High-land bon-nets on their heads, And clay-mores bright and clear, They
left their bon-nie High-land hills, Their wives and bairn-ies dear, To
there were mon-y beat-ing hearts, And mon-y a hope and fear; And

Char-lie came to our ___ town, The _ young _ che-va-lier.
a' the folk cam' rin-nin' out To _ meet the _ che-va-lier.
cam' to fight for Scot-land's right And the young _ che-va-lier. Oh!
draw the sword for Scot-land's lord, The _ young _ che-va-lier.
mon-y were the prayers put up for the young _ che-va-lier.

Char-lie is my dar-ling, my dar-ling, my dar-ling! Oh,

Char-lie is my dar-ling, the young che-va-lier.

Scotland

A HIGHLAND LAD
MY LOVE WAS BORN

Words by Robert Burns
Folk Melody, "The White Cockade"

1. A — High-land lad my — love was born, The
Law-land laws — he — held in scorn; But he still was faith - fu'
to his clan, My — gal - lant — braw John — High-land-man.) Sing
hey, my braw John High-land-man, Sing ho, my braw John —
High-land-man; There's — no' a lad — in — a' the lan' Was —
match — wi' — my — John — High - land - man.

2. With his phi - la - beg and — tar - tan plaid, and
gude clay - more — down by his side. The — la - dies' hearts — he
did tre - pan, my — gal - lant — braw John — High-land-man.) Sing

3. They — ban - ished him be - yond the sea, but
ere the bud — was — on the tree. A - doun my cheeks — the
pearls they ran, em - brac - ing — my — John — High-land-man.) Sing

Refrain

Scotland

FLOW GENTLY, SWEET AFTON

Words by Robert Burns
Melody by Alexander Hume

1. Flow gen - tly, sweet __ Af - ton, a -
2. How loft - y, sweet __ Af - ton, thy
3. Thy crys - tal stream, __ Af - ton, how

mang thy green braes, flow gen - tly, I'll
neigh - bor - ing hills, far mark'd with the
love - ly it glides, and winds by the

sing thee a song in thy praise; My
cours - es of clear, wind - ing rills. There
cot where my Ma - ry re - sides. How

Ma - ry's a - sleep by the mur - mur - ing
dai - ly I __ wan - der as noon ris - es
wan - ton thy __ wa - ters her snow - y feet

stream, flow gen - tly, sweet Af - ton, dis -
high, my flocks and my Ma - ry's sweet
lave, as, gath - 'ring sweet flow - 'rets, she

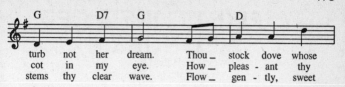

turb not her dream. Thou stock dove whose
cot in my eye. How pleas - ant thy
stems thy clear wave. Flow gen - tly, sweet

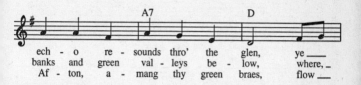

ech - o re - sounds thro' the glen, ye
banks and green val - leys be - low, where,
Af - ton, a - mang thy green braes, flow

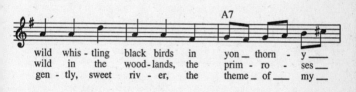

wild whis - tling black birds in yon thorn - y
wild in the wood - lands, the prim - ro - ses
gen - tly, sweet riv - er, the theme of my

den, Thou green crest - ed lap - wing thy
blow. There oft, as mild eve - ning weeps
lays. My Ma - ry's a - sleep by thy

scream - ing for - bear, I charge you, dis -
o - ver the lea, the sweet - scent - ed
mur - mur - ing stream. Flow gen - tly, sweet

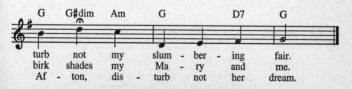

turb not my slum - ber - ing fair.
birk shades my Ma - ry and me.
Af - ton, dis - turb not her dream.

Scotland

MY LUVE IS LIKE A RED, RED ROSE

Words by Robert Burns
Folk Melody, 1745

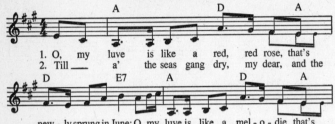

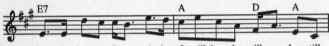

Scotland

WEAVING LILT

Work Song

1. Wait to - day, love, till ___ to - mor - row.
2. Wait to - day un - til ___ to - mor - row.
3. Shuttle I lent the King ___ of France, love,

Ho - ro e - ci - can a - rin hu _ o,
Ho - ro e - ci - can a - rin hu _ o.
Ho - ro e - ci - can a - rin hu _ o.

While I weave fine lin - en for thee, love,
Sown is the lint, but och, will it grow, love?
Loom, it grows in the wood of St. Pat - rick,

Lin - en for thee, fine lin - en for thee, love,
Lin - en for thee, fine lin - en for thee, love,
Shut - tle, nor loom, have I ___ to weave, yet

While ___ I weave fine lin - en for thee, love,
Sure will it grow fine lin - en for thee, love?
wait till I weave fine lin - en for thee, love.

Wait to - day, love, till ___ to - mor - row.
Wait to - day, love, till ___ to - mor - row.
Wait to - day, love, till ___ to - mor - row.

Scotland

OH ROWAN TREE

Words by Lady Carolina Nairne
Folk Melody

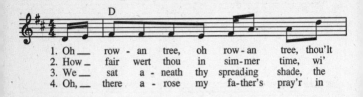

1. Oh __ row - an tree, oh row - an tree, thou'lt
2. How __ fair wert thou in sim - mer time, wi'
3. We __ sat a - neath thy spreading shade, the
4. Oh, __ there a - rose my fa - ther's pray'r in

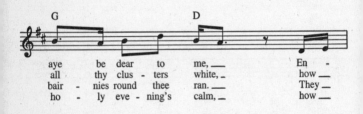

aye be dear to me, __ En __
all thy clus - ters white, __ how __
bair - nies round thee ran. __ They __
ho - ly eve - ning's calm, __ how __

twin'd thou art wi' mo - ny ties, o'
rich and gay thy au - tumn dress, wi'
pu'd thy bon - nie ber - ries red and
sweet was then my mith - er's voice ____

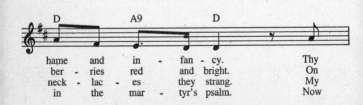

hame and in - fan - cy. Thy
ber - ries red and bright. On
neck - lac - es they strang. My
in the mar - tyr's psalm. Now

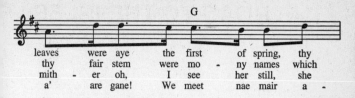

leaves were aye the first of spring, thy
thy fair stem were mo - ny names which
mith - er oh, I see her still, she
a' are gane! We meet nae mair a -

flow'rs the sim - mer's pride; ___ There _
now nae mair ___ I ___ see. ___ But, _
smild our sports _ to ___ see. ___ Wi' _
neath the row - an ___ tree. ___ But _

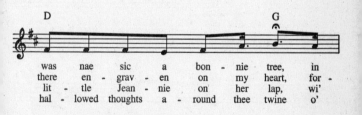

was nae sic a bon - nie tree, in
there en - grav - en on my heart, for -
lit - tle Jean - nie on her lap, wi'
hal - lowed thoughts a - round thee twine o'

Lento

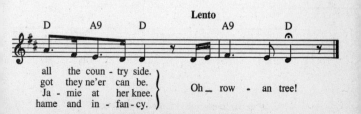

all the coun - try side. }
got they ne'er can be.
Ja - mie at her knee.   Oh_ row - an tree!
hame and in - fan - cy. }

Scotland
THE ROAD TO THE ISLES

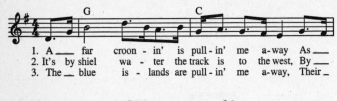

1. A __ far croon-in' is pull-in' me a-way As __
2. It's by shiel wa - ter the track is to the west, By __
3. The __ blue is - lands are pull-in' me a-way, Their __

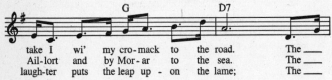

take I wi' my cro-mack to the road. The __
Ail-lort and by Mor-ar to the sea. The __
laugh-ter puts the leap up-on the lame; The __

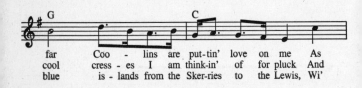

far Coo - lins are put-tin' love on me As
cool cress - es I am think-in' of for pluck And
blue is - lands from the Sker-ries to the Lewis, Wi'

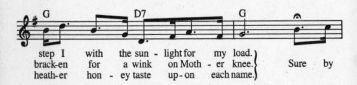

step I with the sun - light for my load.
brack-en for a wink on Moth - er knee. Sure by
heath-er hon - ey taste up-on each name.

Tum-mel and Loch Ran-noch and Loch-a-ber I will go, by __

181

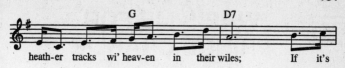

heath-er tracks wi' heav-en in their wiles; If it's

think-in' in your in-ner heart the brag-gart's in my step, You've

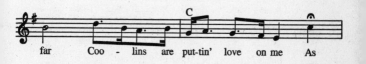

nev-er smelled the tan - gle o' the Isles. Oh the

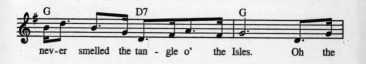

far Coo - lins are put-tin' love on me As

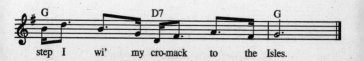

step I wi' my cro-mack to the Isles.

Scotland

WAE'S ME FOR
PRINCE CHARLIE

Words by William Glen, c. 1825
Folk Melody

1. A wee bird cam' to our ha' door, He war-bled sweet and clear-ly, An' aye the o'er-come o' his sang Was "Wae's me for Prince Char-lie!" Oh!
2. Quoth I, "My bird, my bon-nie, bon-nie bird, is that a sang ye bor-row? Are those some words ye've learnt by heart, or a lift o' dool an' sor-row? "Oh!
3. On hills that are by right his ain, he roves a lane-ly stran-ger, on ev-'ry side he's press'd by want, on ev-'ry side is dan-ger. Yes-
4. Dark night cam' on, the temp-est roar'd loud o'er the hills an' val-leys. An' where was't that your Prince lay down, wha's name should been a pal-ace? He
5. But now the bird saw some red coats, an' he shook his wings wi' an-ger. "Oh, this is no a land for me, I'll ta-ry here nae lang-er!" He

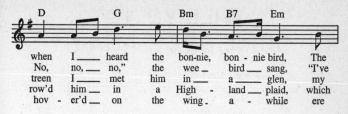

D		G		Bm	B7	Em

when I ____ heard the bon-nie, bon - nie bird, The
No, no, no," the wee __ bird __ sang, "I've
treen I ____ met him in __ a ____ glen, my
row'd him __ in a High - land __ plaid, which
hov - er'd __ on the wing __ a - while ere

A7		Cm		G6	G#dim	D

tears cam' drap - pin rare - ly, I
flown sin' morn - in' ear - ly. But
heart maist bur - stit fair - ly. For
cov - er'd him but spare - ly, an'
he de - part - ed fair - ly But

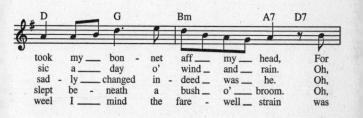

D		G		Bm	A7	D7

took my __ bon - net aff __ my __ head, For
sic a ____ day o' wind __ and __ rain. Oh,
sad - ly ____ changed in - deed __ was __ he. Oh,
slept be - neath a bush __ o' __ broom. Oh,
weel I ____ mind the fare - well __ strain was

G		Em	A7	D9		G

weel I lo'ed ____ Prince __ Char - lie!
wae's me for ____ Prince __ Char - lie!
wae's me for ____ Prince __ Char - lie!
wae's me for ____ Prince __ Char - lie!
"Wae's me for ____ Prince __ Char - lie!

Scotland

WILL YE NO'
COME BACK AGAIN?

1. Bon - nie Char-lie's now a - wa, Safe - ly owre the
2. Mon-y a trait - or 'mang the isles, brak the band o'
3. Mon-y a gal - lant sod - ger faught, mon-y a gal - lant
4. When-e'er I hear the black-bird sing, un-to the eve - ning
5. Sweet the lav'-rock's note and lang, lilt - ing wild-ly

friend - ly __ main; Mon-y a heart will break in twa,
na - ture's __ laws. Mon-y a trait - or wi' his wiles,
chief did __ fa'. Death __ it - self were clear - ly bought,
sink - ing __ down. Or merl that makes the woods to ring,
up the __ glen. And aye the o'er-word o' the sang.

Should he no' come back a - gain.
sought to wear his life a - wa.
a' for Scot - land's King and law.
to me they hae no oth - er sound.
"Will he no' come back a - gain?"

Chorus

Will ye no' come back a - gain? Will ye no' come

back __ a - gain? Bet - ter lo'ed ye

can - na be, Will ye no' come back a - gain?

Scotland

YE BANKS AND BRAES O' BONNIE DOON

Words by Robert Burns
Melody attributed to Charles Miller, 1788

1. Ye banks and braes __ o' bon - nie Doon, __ How can __ ye bloom __ sae fresh and fair? How can ye chant, __ ye lit tle birds, __ and I __ sae wear - y, fu' __ o' care! Ye'll break my heart, __ ye war - bling bird, __ That wan - tons through __ the flow - 'ring thorn, Ye mind me o' __ de - part - ed joys, __ De - part - ed nev - er to __ re - turn.

2. Oft ha'e I roved __ by bon - nie Doon, __ to see __ the rose __ and wood - bine twine. And il - ka bird __ sang o' __ it's luve, __ and fond - ly sae __ did I __ o' mine. Wi' light - some heart __ I stretch'd my hand, __ and pu'd __ a rose - bud from __ the tree. But my fause lov - er stole __ the rose, __ and left __ and left __ the thorn __ wi' me.

St. Thomas
WATER IN ME RUM
Drinking Song

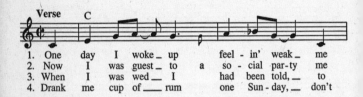

1. One day I woke up feel - in' weak me
2. Now I was guest to a so - cial par - ty me
3. When I was wed I had been told, to
4. Drank me cup of rum one Sun - day, don't

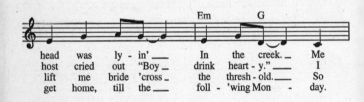

head was ly - in' In the creek. Me
host cried out "Boy drink heart - y. I
lift me bride 'cross the thresh - old. So
get home, till the foll - 'wing Mon - day.

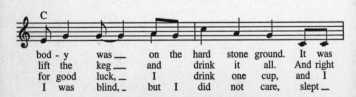

bod - y was on the hard stone ground. It was
lift the keg and drink it all. And right
for good luck, I drink one cup, and I
I was blind, but I did not care, slept

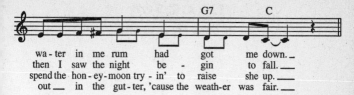

water in me rum had got me down. _
then I saw the night be - gin to fall. _
spend the hon-ey-moon try-in' to raise she up. _
out _ in the gut-ter, 'cause the weath-er was fair. _

Chorus

Wa - ter in me rum was what I found. _

Wa - ter in me rum was what I found. _

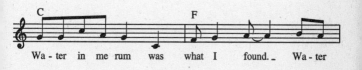

Wa - ter in me rum was what I found. _ Wa - ter

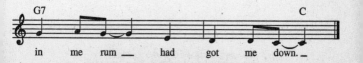

in me rum _ had got me down. _

Serbia

PJESMA
(Come, My Dearest)

Sun - ce ___ žar - ko ___
Tell me my ___ love, what ___

ne si - jaš ___ jed - na - ko
brought on such ___ great sor - row?

sun - ce žar - ko (i - me mo - je)
Do you fear the love I give ___ you,

ne si - jaš ___ jed - na - ko.
love you will ___ not bor - row?

Slovakia

PÁSOL JANKO
(Fields Fair)

1. Pá - sol Jan - ko dva vo - ly u há - ja.
2. Daj nám, Jan - ko, ha - le - nu, u há - ja.
3. Ja vám ha - le - nu ne - dám, u há - ja.
4. Tak sa o - ni jed - na - li, u há - ja.

1. Yan - ko's cat - tle grazed up - on fields _ fair.
2. Ma - gi-strates are com - ing through, fields _ fair.
3. Yan - ko looks up - on the green fields _ fair.
4. Yan - ko's bo - dy lies there on fields _ fair.

Pá - sol Jan - ko dva vo - ly u há - ja.
Daj vám Jan - ko ha - le - nu, u há - ja.
Ja vám ha - le - nu ne - dám, u há - ja.
Tak sa o - ni jed - na - li, u há - ja.

Yan - ko's cat - tle grazed up - on fields _ fair.
Two men plot - ting as they view fields _ fair.
Faced the men with mo - tive seen, fields _ fair.
Ma - gi-strates and live-stock gone, fields _ fair.

Pá - sol Jan - ko dva vo - ly na ze - le-nom ú - ho - ri.
Daj nám Jan - ko ha - le - nu, spá - sol si nam d'a - te - l'u.
Tak sa o - ni jed - na - li, az Ja - ni - ka za - bi - li.
Yan - ko had his cat - tle graze where sweet flow-ers light the days.
"Pay us now," they did de - mand, "or take up and leave this land."
"You'll not put me on my way, for these lands I will not pay.
Tho' he's passed, his cour-age shows, rest - ing mid the bloom-ing rose.

Na - ze - le - nom ú - ho - rí. Ú há - ja.
Spá - sol si nam d'a - te - l'u. Ú há - ja.
Ja sa va - mi po - jed - nám. Ú há - ja.
Az Ja - ni - ka za - bi - li. Ú há - ja.
Where sweet flow-ers light the days. Fields _ fair.
Or take up and leave this land." Fields _ fair.
For these lands I will not pay." Fields _ fair.
Rest - ing mid the bloom-ing rose. Fields _ fair.

Spain
A LA NANITA NANA
(Hear Lullabies and Sleep Now)

1. A la na - ni - ta na - na, na - ni - ta
2. Ma - no - ji - to de ro - sas y de a - le -
3. Pa - ja - ri - llos y fuen - tes, au - ras y
1. Hear lul - la - bies and sleep now, yes, go to
2. My lit - tle bunch of ros - es, with face be -
3. Birds call - ing, foun - tains rush - ing, and blow - ing

e - a, na - ni - ta e - a,
lí - es y de a - le - lí - es,
bri - sas, au - ras y bri - sas:
sleep now, yes, go to sleep.
guil - ing, with face be - guil - ing,
breez - es, and blow - ing breez - es:

Mi Je - sús tie - ne sue - ño, ben - di - to
Qué es lo que es - tás so - ñan - do, qué te son -
Re - pe - tad e - se sue - ño y e - sas son -
My sleep - y Je - sus, may God your slum - ber
What are you dream - ing now, that I see you
Re - peat this smil - ing dream as my ba - by

se - a, ben - di - to se - a. }
ri - es, qué te son - ri - es? }
ri - sas, y e - sas son - ri - sas.
keep, God your slum - ber keep.
smil - ing, I see you smil - ing. }
pleas - es, my ba - by pleas - es.

Fuen - te - ci - illa que cor - res
Hear how the foun - tain bab - bles,

cla - ra y so - no - ra, Rui - se - ñor de la
splash - ing its wa - ters. Night - in - gales in the

sel - va, can - tan - do llo - ras;
woods call all sons and daugh - ters.

{ ca - llad mien-tras la cu - na se ba - lan-
Cuál - es son tus en - sue - ños? di - lo al - ma
{ Rest as the cra - dle calms you now with its
{ What do you see in dream - land? Tell me, my

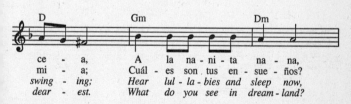

ce - a; A la na - ni - ta na - na,
mi - a; Cuál - es son tus en - sue - ños?
swing - ing; Hear lul - la - bies and sleep now,
dear - est. What do you see in dream - land?

na - ni - ta e - a.
di - lo al - ma mi - a.
while I am sing - ing.
Tell me, my dear - est.

Spain

A UN NIÑO CIEGOCITO
(Unto a Poor Blind Lover)

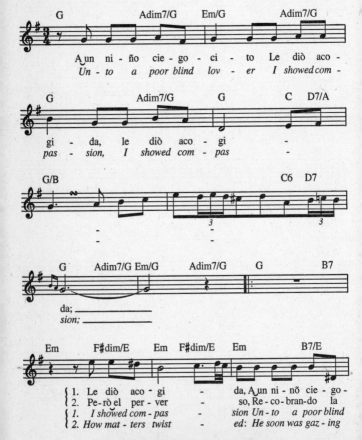

A un ni - ño cie - go - ci - to Le diò aco -
Un - to a poor blind lov - er I showed com -

gi - da, le diò aco - gi -
pas - sion, I showed com - pas -

Pe - rò el per - ver - so, Re - co - bran - do la
How mat - ters twist - ed: He soon was gaz - ing

da; _____
sion; _____

{ 1. Le diò aco - gi - da, A un ni - ño cie - go - so,
{ 2. Pe - rò el per - ver - so, Re - co - bran - do la
{ 1. I showed com - pas - sion Un - to a poor blind
{ 2. How mat - ters twist - ed: He soon was gaz - ing

Spain

CANCIÓN DE MAJA
(May Song)
Andalusia

1. De que sir - ve à las U - si - as
2. Un se - ñor cur - ra - ta - qui - llo
1. *Fool - ish lov - ers, cease to lan - guish,*
2. *Sil - ly fel - lows, vain your pas - sion,*

Ca - me - lar à_____ lo se - ñor,
Me quie - re á_____ mi jon - ja - bar,
Cease to wear - y_____ and com - plain.
Dan - gling round me_____ ev - 'ry - where,

Si ca - ra - cen de zan - dun - ga
Y se vis - te de mil mo - dós
Leave your sigh - ing, leave your an - guish,
Dressed in all the lat - est fash - ion,

A la me - jor_____ o - ca - sion?
Pa - ra po - der - me agra - dar.
Nought to me a - vails your_____ pain.
Such con - ceits I_____ can - not_____ bear.

A - si di ma - jo - ta Quie - ro siem - pre an -
To - do es dar sal - ti - tos Los pies ar - ra -
All your wiles ig - nor - ing, Free as bird I'm
Such fan - tas - tic pa - cing, Bow - ing and grim -

dar, Que es el ma - ne - ji - llo
strar, Re - frun - cir la bo - ca,
soar - ing, All your sweet al - lure - ments
a - cing, Emp - ty flat - tering speech - es,

Sweden

NECKEN'S POLSKA
(On a Crystal Throne)
Words by A.A. Afzelius
Folk Melody

Dm | A7 | Dm | C/E

1. Djupt i haf - vet på de - man - te - häl - len
2. Ä - girs dött - trar ho - nom sak - te - li - ga
3. O hvar dväljs du, kla - ra - ste bland stjer - nor!
1. *On a crys - tal throne, be - neath the o - cean,*
2. *"Why do you still gleam, nor heed my yearn - ing,*
3. *So he sang, and then, in high - est glo - ry,*

Dm/F | Gm6 | A7 | Dm

Nec - ken hvi - lar i grö - nan sal.
Gun - ga fram pa den kla - ra sjö.
I den bla - nan - de skym - ning-sstund?
Nec - ken dreams in his deep green hall,
Star that shines while the world's a sleep,
dis - tant Fre - ya shone through the night.

A7 | Bb7 | Dm | C/E

Nat - tens tär - nor spän - na mör - ka pel - len
Har - pans ljud de gå så sor - ge - li - ga.
Du, som for - dom, en af jor - aens tär - nor.
As he pon - ders, lost in his e - mo - tion,
You that once, when Earth's first fires were burn - ing,
As she lis - tened to his mourn - ful sto - ry,

Dm/F | Gm6 | A7 | Dm

Öf - ver skog, öf - ver berg och dal.
Sö - ka fjerr - an en vag att dö.
Var min brud u - ti haf - vets grund.
Shades of eve - ning soft - ly fall.
Were my bride in the sha - dowy deep,
all his tears she saw in the light.

Sweden
VERMELAND
Words by A. Frysell, c. 1850
Folk Melody, Seventeenth Century

1. Ack Ver - me - land, du skö - na, du herr - li - ga land! Du kro - na för Sve - a - ri - kes län - der! Ja, om jag kom - me midt i det för - lof - va - de land, Till Verm - land jag än - då å - ter land,

2. Ja! när du en - gang skall bort och gift - a - dig, min vän, Da skall du till Ver - me - land fa - ra; Der fin - nes nog guds gaf - vor med flick - or qvar i - gen, och al - la ä de präk - ti - ga och

1. *Oh! Ver - me - land, my dear - est, my fair - est do - main, Bright gem with - in the shin - ing crown of Swe - den. The om I come to life again in that promised land, To Vermland I'll return.*

2. *Oh, how I hope and pray that my love is ev - er true and that her vow to me is still un - bro - ken. For ev - 'ry day that pass - es, I claim my vow a - new; I hold it as the high - est words I've*

vän - der. _____ Ja, der ___ vill jag
ra - ra. _____ Men fri - ar du
E - den. _____ Here rocked _ once my
spo - ken. _____ My love for her and

lef - va, ja, der ___ vill jag dö; Och
der ___ sa var mun - ter och glad! Ty
cra - dle, and here shall bloom my grave; And
Verme - land is all that holds my heart, and

en - gång i - från Verm - land jug
mun - tra gos - sar vil - ja Verm -
here the sweet - est maid - en her
if I find my way back home, we

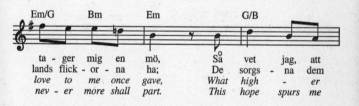

ta - ger mig en mö, Så vet jag, att
lands flick - or - na ha; De sorgs - na dem
love to me once gave, What high - er
nev - er more shall part. This hope spurs me

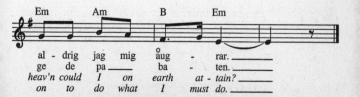

al - drig jag mig åug - rar. _____
ge de pa ___ ba - ten. _____
heav'n could I on earth at - tain? _____
on to do what I must do. _____

Syria

AÏNTE
(Sleep, My Child)
Smyrna

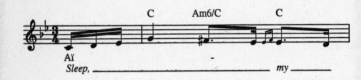

Aï -
Sleep, _____ my _____

nte. aï - nte koi mē - sou, Ko - rē
child, my pret - ty one, _____ and soft - ly

mou. K'é - gó, ___ k'é-gó nà soū _____
dream. Cai - ro _____ in rice I'll make _____

_____ cha - ri - so tēn A - le -
_____ and give _____ you. All A - lex -

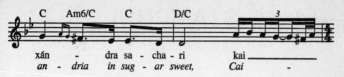

xán - dra sa - cha - ri kai _____
an - dria in sug - ar sweet, Cai -

tò _____ kai tò Mi-sè - ri ri -
ro _____ in rice, in hon - ey all _____ the _____

si, Kai tèn Kon - stan - ti - nou - po -
Nile, For you Con - stan - ti - no -

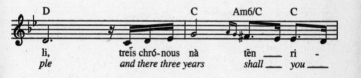

li, treîs chró-nous nà tèn _____ ri -
ple and there three years shall _____ you _____

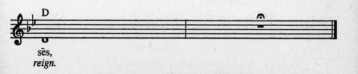

sēs,
reign.

Tripoli
STABOUL

French Words after V. Bérard
Melody attributed to Si Mohammed Said

1. Ah! _____ Stam - boul
2. Ah! _____ Tous les -
1. Ah! _____ Stam - boul
2. Ah! _____ All these

lè - ve sa ban - niè - re Et ses
son - ges de la _____ gloi - re Sont sor -
rais - es her ban - ner _____ fly - ing, To the
striv - ings for fame and _____ glo - ry Call me

peu - ples _____ pour la guer - re Dé -
tis de _____ ma mé - moi - re, Je _____
war go _____ all her peo - ple, March - ing
vain - ly _____ from my dream - ing, All I

fi - lent _____ au bruit du _____ tam - bour Ab - dul
ne peux _____ rê - ver _____ qu'a - mour Pour ma
brave - ly _____ to the sound _____ of the drums. For the
long for _____ is the kiss _____ of my love. For my

203

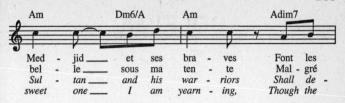

Am   **Dm6/A**   **Am**   **Adim7**

Med - jid ___ et ses bra - ves   Font les
bel - le ___ sous ma ten - te   Mal - gré
Sul - tan ___ and his war - riors   Shall de -
sweet one ___ I am yearn - ing,   Though the

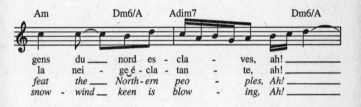

Am   **Dm6/A**   **Adim7**   **Dm6/A**

gens du ___ nord es - cla - ves, ah! ___
la nei - ge é - cla - tan - te, ah! ___
feat the ___ North - ern peo - ples, Ah! ___
snow - wind ___ keen is blow - ing, Ah! ___

Moi je
Mon cœur
But I
burns my

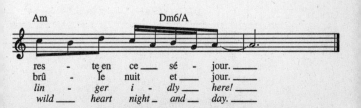

Am   **Dm6/A**

res - te en ce ___ sé - jour. ___
brû - le nuit et ___ jour. ___
lin - ger i - dly ___ here! ___
wild ___ heart night ___ and ___ day. ___

Tunis

SOLEÏMA

Anonymous French Words, after Mourakkich

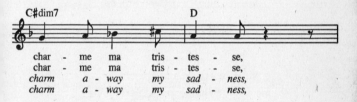
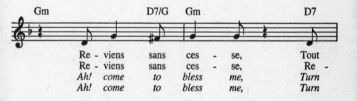

Turkey

CHARKI HIDJAZ

(The Sun Hangs High)

Her né_ rut - bé____ if - ti - har___ it_
The sun_ hangs_ high___ in thburn - ing__ noon,

sem - dé chim - di____ va - r yé - ri.____
and my soul_ thirsts_ for you__ with de - sire.____

E - y - lé - di - ni - h_ ya - sé - ra - pa - y
O mybe - lov - ed!___ see_ all my_ sor - row,

du - n ghi - djé_ bou____ ké - m - té - ri.____
hear_ now the plead - ing_____ of_ my_ heart.___

Sé - v - mé - mé_ kka - bil o_ lour - mou
Be_ now my moon ___ of_ sil - ver___ splen - dor,

sén ghu - lu - na - zi - k té - ri _____
Shed up - on _ me _ your ra - di - ant _ glo - ry.

Sé - v - mé - mék ka - bil o - lou - r - mou
Low - ly _ I _ wor - ship you _ from _ a - far,

sen ghu - lu - na - zi - k té - ri _____
Though with an - guish _____ I _____ am _ bro - ken.

E - y - lé - di - ni - h - ya _ sé - ra - pa _ y
O - my - be - lov - ed! see _ all my _ sor - row,

du - n ghi - djé - bou _____ ké - m - té - ri. _____
hea mo we the plead - ing _____ of _ my _ heart. _____

United States of America

BLACK IS THE COLOR OF MY TRUE LOVE'S HAIR

Southern Appalachia

Black, black, black is the col-or of my true love's hair.

1. Her lips _____ are like a rose so fair. And the pret-ti-est face and the neat-est _____ hands. I love _____ the grass where-on she stands,
2. Her face _____ is some-thing tru-ly rare. Oh I do love my love and so well _____ she _____ knows, I love _____ the ground where-on she goes,
3. A-lone, _____ my life would be so bare. I would sigh, I would weep, I would nev-er fall a-sleep. My love _____ is way be-yond com-pare,

she with the won-drous hair.

United States of America

THE BLUE TAIL FLY

(Jimmy Crack Corn)

Folk version of a minstrel song by Dan Emmett
(Emmett's song was published in 1846)

1. When I was young, I used to wait on
2. He used to ride each af-ter-noon, I'd
3. The po-ny jump, he run, he pitch, he
4. Old mas-ter's dead and gone to rest, they
5. A skeet-er bites right through your clothes, a

mas-ter, hand-ing him his plate. I brought his bot-tle when
fol-low with a hick-'ry broom. The po-ny kicked his
threw my mas-ter in the ditch. My mas-ter died and
say it hap-pened for the best, I won't for-get un -
hor-net strikes you on the nose, the bees may get you

he was dry and brushed a-way the blue-tail fly.)
legs up high, when bit-ten by the blue-tail fly.
who'll de-ny, the blame was on the blue-tail fly.
til I die my mas-ter and the blue-tail fly.
pass-ing by, but oh much worse, the blue-tail fly.

Chorus

Jim-my crack corn and I don't care, Jim-my crack corn and

I don't care, Jim-my crack corn and

I don't care, old mas-ter's gone a-way.

United States of America

BURY ME NOT ON THE LONE PRAIRIE

Cowboy Ballad, c. 1870s
Attributed to H. Clemens
Based on "The Ocean Burial" (1849)
Words by the Rev. Edwin H. Chapin
Music by Ossian N. Dodge

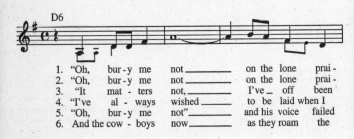

1. "Oh, bur-y me not_____ on the lone prai-
2. "Oh, bur-y me not_____ on the lone prai-
3. "It mat-ters not,_____ I've off been
4. "I've al-ways wished_____ to be laid when I
5. "Oh, bur-y me not"_____ and his voice failed
6. And the cow-boys now_____ as they roam the

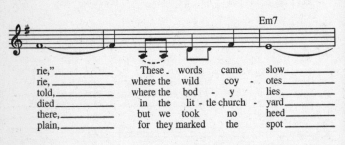

rie,"_____ These words came slow_____
rie,_____ where the wild coy-otes_____
told,_____ where the bod-y lies_____
died,_____ in the lit-tle church-yard_____
there,_____ but we took no heed_____
plain,_____ for they marked the spot_____

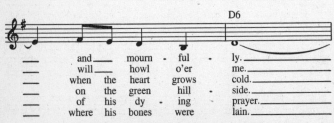

___ and_ mourn-ful-ly._____
___ will_ howl o'er me._____
___ when the heart grows cold._____
___ on the green hill-side._____
___ of his dy-ing prayer._____
___ where his bones were lain.

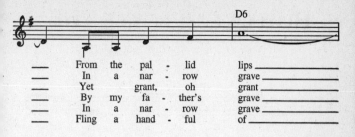

From the pal - lid lips _____
In a nar - row grave _____
Yet grant, oh grant _____
By my fa - ther's grave _____
In a nar - row grave _____
Fling a hand - ful of _____

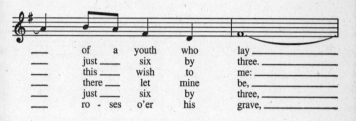

of a youth who lay _____
just ___ six by three. _____
this ___ wish to me: _____
there ___ let mine be, _____
just ___ six by three, _____
ro - ses o'er his grave, _____

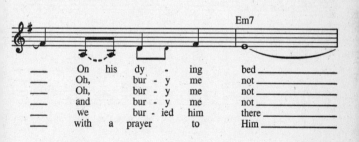

On his dy - ing bed _____
Oh, bur - y me not _____
Oh, bur - y me not _____
and bur - y me not _____
we bur - ied him there _____
with a prayer to Him _____

at the close of day.
on the lone prai - rie."
on the lone prai - rie."
on the lone prai - rie."
on the lone prai - rie.
who his soul will save.

United States of America
CLEMENTINE
Mining Song, probably from California
Attributed to Percy Montrose, 1863 or 1883

1. In a cav - ern, in a can - yon, Ex - ca-
2. Light she was, and like a fai - ry, and her
3. Drove she duck - lings to the wa - ter ev - 'ry
4. Ru - by lips a - bove the wa - ter, blow - ing

vat - ing for a mine, Dwelt a min - er, for - ty-
shoes were num - ber nine. Her - ring box - es with - out
morn - ing just at nine. Hit her foot a - gainst a
bub - bles soft and fine. Alas for me! I was no

nin - er, And his daugh - ter, Clem - en - tine.
top - ses, san - dals were for Clem - en - tine.
splin - ter, fell in - to the foam - ing brine.
swim - mer, so I lost my Clem - en - tine.

Chorus
Oh my

dar - ling, oh my dar - ling, oh my dar - ling Clem - en -

tine. You are lost and gone for -

ev - er, dread - ful sor - ry, Clem - en - tine.

United States of America

THE CRUEL WAR IS RAGING

Civil War

1. The cruel war is rag-ing, John-ny has to fight. I want to be with him from morn - ing till night. I want to be with him. It grieves my heart so.
2. I'd go to your cap-tain, get down on my knees, and ten - thou-sand gold gui-neas I'd give for your re - lease. Ten - thou - sand gold gui - neas, it grieves my heart so
3. To-mor-row is Sun-day, Mon-day is the day, that your cap - tain will call you, and you must o - bey. Your cap - tain will call you, it grieves my heart so.
4. I'll tie back my hair, men's cloth - ing I'll put on, and I'll pass as your com - rade as we march a - long. I'll pass as your com - rade, no one will ev - er know.
5. Oh, John - ny, oh, John - ny, I fear you are un - kind, for I love you far bet - ter than all of man - kind. I love you far bet - ter than words can e'er ex - press.

Won't you let me go with you? (1.-4.) No, my love, no.
(5.) Yes, my love, yes.

United States of America

DEEP RIVER

African-American Spiritual

Deep _____ Riv - er, my home is o - ver

Jor - dan, Deep _____ Riv - er, Lord, I

want to cross o - ver in - to camp - ground.

Oh, don't you want to go o - ver to that gos - pel

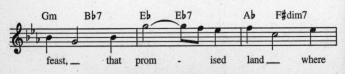

feast, _____ that prom - ised land _____ where

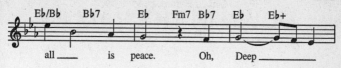

all ___ is peace. Oh, Deep ___

Riv - er, my home is o - ver Jor - dan,

Deep ___ Riv - er, Lord, I

want to cross o - ver in - to camp - ground. I

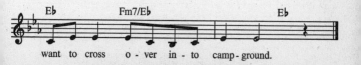

want to cross o - ver in - to camp - ground.

United States of America

DOWN IN THE VALLEY

Nineteenth Century
Words by an anonymous inmate at Raleigh State Prison

1. Down in the valley, valley so low, _____ late in the eve-ning hear the train blow. _____ Hear that train blow-ing, hear that train blow; _____ hang your head o-ver hear that train blow. _____

2. Ro-ses love sun-shine, vi-'lets love dew, _____ an-gels in heav-en know I love you. _____ Know I love you, dear, know I love you, _____ An-gels in heav-en know I love you. _____

3. Write me a let-ter, send it by mail; _____ send it in care of Bir-ming-ham jail. _____ Bir-ming-ham jail-house, Bir-ming-ham jail, _____ send it in care of Bir-ming-ham jail. _____

United States of America

HE'S GOT THE WHOLE
WORLD IN HIS HANDS

African-American Folksong
possibly from North Carolina

United States of America

THE DRUNKEN SAILOR

Sea Chanty

'Way hay, 'n'up she ris - es!

Pat - ent blocks o' dif - f'rent siz - es,

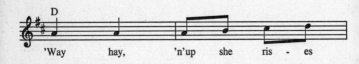

'Way hay, 'n'up she ris - es

Ear - lye in the morn - in'!

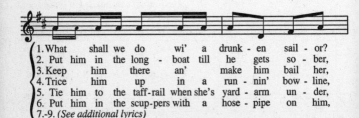

1. What shall we do wi' a drunk - en sail - or?
2. Put him in the long - boat till he gets so - ber,
3. Keep him there an' make him bail her,
4. Trice him up in a run - nin' bow - line,
5. Tie him to the taff - rail when she's yard - arm un - der,
6. Put him in the scup - pers with a hose - pipe on him,
7.-9. *(See additional lyrics)*

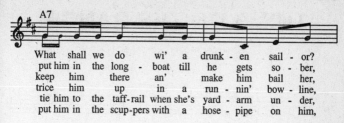

A7

What shall we do wi' a drunk - en sail - or?
put him in the long - boat till he gets so - ber,
keep him there an' make him bail her,
trice him up in a run - nin' bow - line,
tie him to the taff-rail when she's yard - arm un - der,
put him in the scup-pers with a hose - pipe on him,

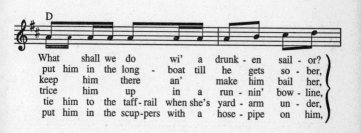

D

What shall we do wi' a drunk - en sail - or?
put him in the long - boat till he gets so - ber,
keep him there an' make him bail her,
trice him up in a run - nin' bow - line,
tie him to the taff - rail when she's yard - arm un - der,
put him in the scup-pers with a hose - pipe on him,

A7   D

Ear - lye in the morn - in'!

Additional Lyrics

7. Take him an' shake 'im, an' try an' wake 'im,
   Earlye in the mornin'!

8. Give him a dose o' salt an' water,
   Earlye in the mornin'!

9. Give him a taste o' the bosun's rope-end,
   Earlye in the mornin'!

United States of America
HOME ON THE RANGE
Kansas, c. 1873
Attributed to Dr. Brewster Higley (words) and Dan Kelly (music)

1. Oh, give me a home where the buf-fa-lo roam, Where the deer and the an-te-lope play, _____ Where sel-dom is heard a dis-cour-ag-ing word, And the skies are not cloud-y all

2. How oft-en at night when the heav-ens are bright with the light from the glit-ter-ing stars, _____ have I stood there a-mazed and asked as I gazed, if their glo-ry ex-ceeds that of

3. Where the air is so pure, the _____ zeph-yrs so free, the _____ breez-es so balm-y and light. _____ That I would not ex-change my _____ home on the range for _____ all of the cit-ies so

4. Oh, I love those wild flow'rs in this dear land of ours. The _____ cur-lew, I love to hear scream. And I love the white rocks and the an-te-lope flocks, that _____ graze on the moun-tain-tops

day. _____
ours. _____
bright. _____
green. _____

Home,

home   on   the   range, _____   Where the

deer   and   the   an - te - lope   play. _____

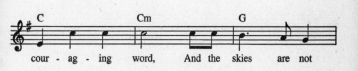

_____   Where   sel - dom   is   heard   a   dis -

cour - ag - ing   word,   And the   skies   are not

D7   G
cloud - y   all   day. _____

United States of America

HOW CAN I KEEP
FROM SINGING

Folk Hymn

1. My life flows on in end-less song a-
2. What though the temp-est round me rears, I
3. When ty-rants trem-ble, sick with fear And

bove earth's lam-en-ta-tion. I hear the real, though
know the truth, it liv-eth. What though the dark-ness
hear their death knells ring-ing; When friends re-joice both

far off hymn that hails a new cre-a-tion. No
round me close, Songs in the nights it giv-eth. No
far and near, How can I keep from sing-ing? In

storm can shake my in-most calm while to that rock I'm
storm can shake my in-most calm while to that rock I'm
pris-on cell and dun-geon vile Our thoughts to them are

cling-ing. It sounds an ech-o___
cling-ing. Since love is lord of___
wing-ing. When friends by shame are___

in my soul. }
Heav'n and earth, } How can I keep from sing-ing?
un-de-filed, }

United States of America

HUSH, LITTLE BABY

Carolinas

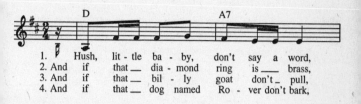

1. Hush, lit-tle ba-by, don't say a word,
2. And if that __ dia-mond ring is __ brass,
3. And if that __ bil-ly goat don't __ pull,
4. And if that __ dog named Ro-ver don't bark,

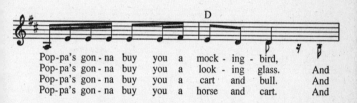

Pop-pa's gon-na buy you a mock-ing-bird,
Pop-pa's gon-na buy you a look-ing glass. And
Pop-pa's gon-na buy you a cart and bull. And
Pop-pa's gon-na buy you a horse and cart. And

If that mock-ing-bird don't sing
if that look-ing glass gets broke,
if that cart and bull turn o-ver
if that horse and cart fall down,

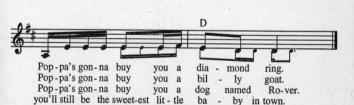

Pop-pa's gon-na buy you a dia-mond ring.
Pop-pa's gon-na buy you a bil-ly goat.
Pop-pa's gon-na buy you a dog named Ro-ver.
you'll still be the sweet-est lit-tle ba-by in town.

United States of America

JACOB'S LADDER

African-American Spiritual from the South,
Seventeenth or Eighteenth Century

United States of America

RED RIVER VALLEY

Nineteenth Century

1. Come and sit by my side if you love me, ___
2. Won't you think of this val - ley you're leav - ing, ___
3. From this val - ley they say you are go - ing. ___
4. I have prom - ised you, dar - ling, that nev - er ___

___ Do not has - ten to bid me a -
___ oh, how lone - ly, how sad it will
___ When you go, may your dar - ling go,
___ will a word from my lips cause you

dieu, ___ But re - mem - ber the
be. ___ Oh, ___ think of the
too? ___ Would you leave her be -
pain. ___ And my life, it will

Red Riv - er Val - ley, ___ And the
fond heart you're break - ing, ___ and the
hind un - pro - tect - ed ___ when she
be yours for - ev - er, ___ if you

cow - boy that loves you so true. ___
grief you are caus - ing ___ me. ___
loves no ___ oth - er but you? ___
on - ly will love me a - gain. ___

United States of America
SHENANDOAH
Eighteenth or Nineteenth Century

1. Oh, Shen - an - doah, I long to
2. Oh, Shen - an - doah, I love your
3. Oh, Shen - an - doah, I'm bound to

hear you, } { Oh,
daugh-ter, } { For
leave you, } { Oh,

A - way you roll-ing riv - er.

Shen - an - doah I long to hear you.
her I'd cross your roam-ing wa - ter. } A -
Shen - an - doah I'll not de - ceive you.

way, I'm bound a - way, 'Cross the

wide Mis - sou - ri.

United States of America
SIMPLE GIFTS
Shaker Hymn

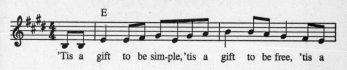

'Tis a gift to be sim-ple, 'tis a gift to be free, 'tis a

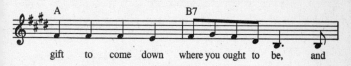

gift to come down where you ought to be, and

when we find our-selves in the place just right, 'twill

be in the val-ley of love and de-light. When true sim-

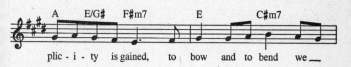

plic-i-ty is gained, to bow and to bend we

won't be a-shamed. To turn, turn will be our de-light till by

turn-ing and turn-ing we come out right.

United States of America

SOMETIMES I FEEL LIKE
A MOTHERLESS CHILD

African-American Spiritual, Slavery Era

1. Some-times I feel like a moth-er-less child,
2. Some-times I feel like I'm al - most gone,

Some-times I feel like a moth-er-less child,
Some-times I feel like I'm al - most gone,

Some-times I feel like a moth-er-less child, A long way_ from
Some-times I feel like I'm al - most gone, Way up in_ the

home,_____ A long way_ from home.
heav'n-ly land, Way up in the heav'n-ly land.

(True be-liev-er.) A long way_ from home,_____ A
(True be-liev-er.) Way up in_ the heav'n-ly land, Way

long way_ from home.
up in the heav'n-ly land._____

United States of America

STEAL AWAY

African-American Spiritual, Slavery Era

United States of America

THE STREETS OF LAREDO

Nineteenth Century
Based on the Irish ballad "A Handful of Laurel"

1. As I was a - walk - in' the streets of La - re - do, As I walked out in La - re - do one day, I spied a young cow - boy all wrapped in white lin - en, All wrapped in white lin - en, and cold as the clay.

2. "I see by your out - fit that you are a cow - boy," these words he did say as I bold - ly walked by. "Come sit down be - side me and hear my sad sto - ry, I'm shot in the breast and I know I must die."

3. "It was once in the sad - dle I used to go dash - ing, once in the sad - dle I used to go gay. First down to Ro - sie's and then to the card house. Got shot in the breast and I'm dy - ing to - day."

4. "Get six - teen gam - blers to car - ry my cof - fin, let six jol - ly cow - boys come sing me a song. Take me to the grave - yard and lay the sod o'er me, for I'm a young cow - boy and I know I've done wrong."

5. "Oh bang the drum slow - ly and play the fife low - ly, ___ play the dead march as you carry me a - long. Put bunch - es of ros - es all o - ver my cof - fin, ___ ro - ses to dead - en the clods as they fall."

United States of America

WAYFARING STRANGER

Southern American Folk Hymn

1. I am a poor___ way-far-ing stran-ger while trav-'ling
2. I know dark clouds ___ will gath-er round me, I know my
3. I'll soon be free ___ from ev-'ry tri - al, my bod - y

through_ this world of woe, Yet there's no sick - ness, toil nor
way ___ is rough and steep; But gol-den fields ___ lie out be-
sleep ___ in the church-yard; I'll drop the cross ___ of self de-

dan-ger in that bright world___ to which I go. I'm go-ing
fore me where God's re - deemed ___ shall ev - er sleep. I'm go-ing
ni - al and en - ter on ___ my great re-ward. I'm go-ing

there _____ to see my Fa - ther, I'm go - ing
there _____ to see my moth - er, She said she'd
there _____ to see my Sav - ior, To sing his

there ___ no more to roam; } I'm on-ly go - ing o-ver
meet ___ me when I come; } I'm on-ly go - ing o-ver
praise ___ for - ev - er-more; }

Jor-dan, I'm on - ly go - ing o - ver home.

United States of America

SWING LOW,
SWEET CHARIOT

African-American Spiritual, Slavery Era

Refrain:

F   Dm   Gm7   C7

Swing low,   sweet cha - ri - ot, ___

Dm   Am   Gm7   C9

Com - ing for to car - ry me home.

F   Bbmaj7   Gm7   C7

Swing low,   sweet cha - ri - ot, ___

F   Bb   F   C   F

Com - ing for to car - ry me home.   { I / If

Bbmaj7   C7

looked o - ver Jor - dan and what did I see?
you ___ get there be - fore ___ I do, ___

Dm   Am   Gm7   C7

Com - in' for to car - ry me home,   A
Com - ing for to car - ry me home,   Tell

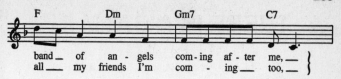

band of an - gels com - ing af - ter me, —
all my friends I'm com - ing too, —

Com-ing for to car - ry me home. home.

Refrain

Swing low, sweet cha - ri - ot, —

Com - ing for to car - ry me home.

Swing low, sweet cha - ri - ot, —

Com - ing for to car - ry me home.

234

United States of America

THERE IS A BALM IN GILEAD

African-American Spiritual, Slavery Era

There — is a balm in

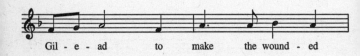

Gil - e - ad to make the wound - ed

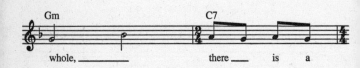

whole, _____ there — is a

balm in Gil - e - ad to

heal the sin - sick soul.

1. Some -
2. Don't
3. If you

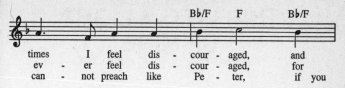

times   I   feel   dis - cour - aged,   and
ev - er feel   dis - cour - aged,   for
can - not preach like   Pe - ter,   if   you

think   my   work's in   vain,   but
Je - sus   is   your   friend,   who,
can - not pray like   Paul,   you can

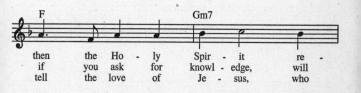

then   the   Ho - ly   Spir - it   re -
if   you   ask   for   knowl - edge,   will
tell   the   love   of   Je - sus,   who

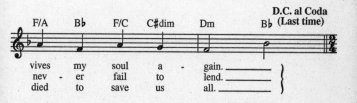

vives   my   soul   a - gain. _____
nev - er   fail   to   lend. _____
died   to   save   us   all. _____

CODA

heal   the sin - sick   soul. _____

United States of America

THIS LITTLE LIGHT OF MINE

African-American Spiritual, Slavery Era

This lit-tle light of mine,— I'm gon-na let it shine,-

— this lit-tle light of mine, —

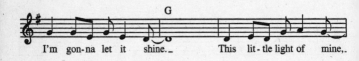

I'm gon-na let it shine.— This lit-tle light of mine,-

— I'm gon-na let it shine — ev-'ry

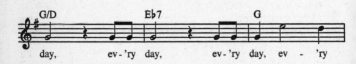

day, ev-'ry day, ev-'ry day, ev-'ry

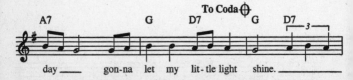

day — gon-na let my lit-tle light shine. —

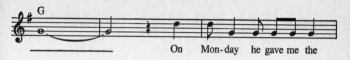

On Mon-day he gave me the

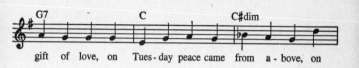

gift of love, on Tues-day peace came from a-bove, on

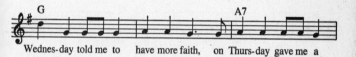

Wednes-day told me to have more faith, on Thurs-day gave me a

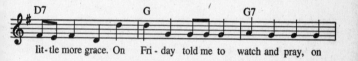

lit-tle more grace. On Fri-day told me to watch and pray, on

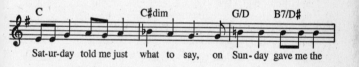

Sat-ur-day told me just what to say, on Sun-day gave me the

pow-er di-vine, just to let my lit-tle light shine.

CODA

shine.

United States of America

WHEN JOHNNY COMES MARCHING HOME

Words and Music by Louis Lambert, 1863
Melody adapted from an Irish Folksong

1. When John-ny comes march-ing home a-gain, hur-rah!___ Hur-rah!___ We'll give him a heart-y wel-come then, hur-rah!___ Hur-rah!___ Oh, the men will cheer and the boys will shout. The la-dies they___ will all turn out. } And we'll all feel gay when John-ny comes march-ing home.

2. Get rea-dy for the Ju-bi-lee, hur-rah!___ Hur-rah!___ We'll give___ the he-ro three times three, hur-rah!___ Hur-rah!___ The___ lau-rel wreath___ is rea-dy now to place up-on___ his loy-al brow. }

3. The old___ church bell will peal with joy, hur-rah!___ Hur-rah!___ To wel-come home our dar-ling boy, hur-rah!___ Hur-rah!___ The___ vil-lage lads___ and las-sies say, with ro-ses they___ will strew the way. }

4. Let love___ and friend-ship on that day, hur-rah!___ Hur-rah!___ Their choic-est treas-ures then dis-play, hur-rah!___ Hur-rah!___ And___ let each one___ per-form some part, to fill with joy___ the war-rior's heart. }

United States of America

WHEN THE SAINTS GO MARCHING IN

New Orleans Gospel Song, possibly originally from the Bahamas
Attributed to Katherine E. Purvis (words)
and James M. Black (music), 1896

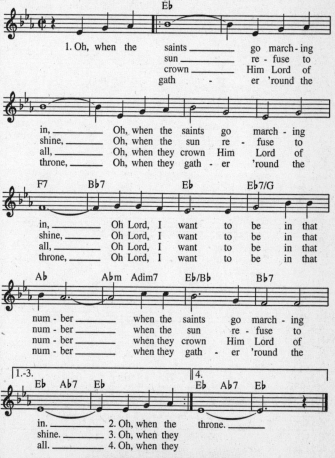

240

United States of America
WONDROUS LOVE
Southern American Folk Hymn,
Seventeenth or Eighteenth Century

| G | Dm | Am7 | F | Am7 | Dm | F |

1. What won-drous love is this, O my soul, O my
2. What won-drous love is this, O my soul, O my
3. To God and to the Lamb I will sing, I will
4. And when from death I'm free, I'll sing on, I'll sing

| Am | F | Am | | F | Am7 |

soul, what won-drous love is this, O my
soul, what won-drous love is this, O my
sing, to God and to the Lamb, I will
on, and when from death I'm free, I'll sing

| Dm | G/B | Am | Dm |

soul! What won-drous love is this that
soul! What won-drous love is this that
sing; to God and to the Lamb who
on; and when from death I'm free, I'll

| Am | F | Dm | G | Dm |

caused the Lord _ of bliss to bear the dread-ful
caused the Lord _ of life to lay a-side his
is the great _ I AM, while mil-lions join the
sing and joy-ful be, and through e-ter-ni-

| F | Am7 | Dm | Am |

curse for my soul, for my soul, to
crown for my soul, for my soul, to
theme I will sing, I will sing; while
ty I'll sing on, I'll sing on, and

| Fmaj7 | C6/G | Am7 | D5 |

bear the dread-ful curse for my soul.
lay a-side his crown for my soul.
mil-lions join the theme I will sing.
through e-ter-ni-ty I'll sing on.

United States of America
YANKEE DOODLE
Revolutionary War

1. Fa - ther and I went down to camp, A -
2. And there we saw a thou - sand men, as
3. There was Cap - tain Wash - ing - ton up -
4. And then the feath - ers on his hat, they
5. We saw a lit - tle bar - rel too, the
6. And there they'd fife a - way like fun, and

long with Cap - tain Good - ing, and there we saw the
rich as Squire Da - vid. And what they was - ted
on a slap - ping stal - lion, a - giv - ing or - ders
looked so 'tar - nel fine, ah! I want - ed pesk - i -
heads were made of leath - er. They knocked on it with
play on corn - stalk fid - dles. And some had rib - bons

men and boys as thick as hast - y pud - ding.
ev - 'ry day, I wish it could be saved.
to his men, I guess it was a mil - lion.
ly to get to give to me Je - mi - ma.
lit - tle clubs and called the folks to - geth - er.
red as blood all bound a - round their mid - dles.

Yan - kee Doo - dle, keep it up, Yan - kee Doo - dle dan - dy,

Mind the mu - sic and the step, and with the girls be hand - y.

Venezuela

DUÉRMETE NIÑO CHIQUITO

(Go to Sleep My Little Baby)

Wales
AR HYD Y NOS
(All through the Night)

1. Holl am - rant - au'r sêr ddy - wed - ant, Ar hyd y
2. O mor sir - iol gwe - na se - ren, Ar hyd y
1. *Love, fear not if sad thy dream - ing All through the*
2. *An - gels watch - ing ev - er round thee All through the*

nos, "Dym - a'r ffordd i fro go - go - niant,"
nos, I ol - en - o'i chwaer - ddae - ar - en,
night, Through o'er - cast, bright stars are gleam - ing
night, In thy slum - bers close sur - round thee

Ar hyd y nos. Gol - en ar - all
Ar hyd y nos. Nos yw he - naint
All through the night. Joy will come to
All through the night. They should of all

yw ty - wyll - wch, I ar - ddaug os gwir bryd - ferth - wch,
pan ddaw cys - tudd, Ond i hardd - u dŷn a'i hwyr - ddydd,
thee at morn - ing, Life with sun - ny hope a - dorn - ing,
fear dis - arm thee, No fore - bod - ings should a - larm thee,

Teu - lu'r nef oedd mewn taw - el - wch, Ar hyd y nos.
Rho'wn ein go - len gwan i'n gi - lydd, Ar hyd y nos.
Though sad dreams may give dark warn - ing All through the night.
They will let no per - il harm thee, All through the night.

Wales

HELA'R 'SGYVARNOG

(Hunting the Hare)

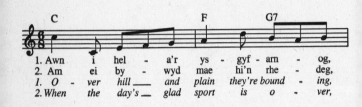

1. Awn i hel - a'r ys - gyf - arn - og
2. Am ei by - wyd mae hi'n rhe - deg,
1. O - ver hill and plain they're bound - ing,
2. When the day's glad sport is o - ver,

Dym - a for - eu hyf - rhd iach;
E - for claw wd a god - rau'r llwyn:
Thro' the air they seem to fly,
Seat - ed in the Bar - on's hall,

Cod - wyd hi ar graig eith - in - og:
We - le fil - gi fel yn he - deg,
Hark! the mer - ry horn is sound - ing,
Round the fes - tive board dis - cov - er,

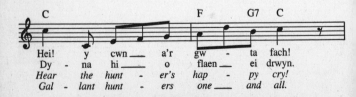

Hei! y cwn a'r gwy - ta fach!
Dy - na hi o flaen ei drwyn.
Hear the hunt - er's hap - py cry!
Gal - lant hunt - ers one and all.

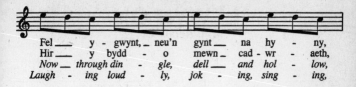

Fel __ y __ gwynt, __ neu'n gynt __ na hy - ny,
Hir __ y bydd - o mewn __ cad - wr - aeth,
Now __ through din - gle, dell __ and hol - low,
Laugh - ing loud - ly, jok - ing, sing - ing,

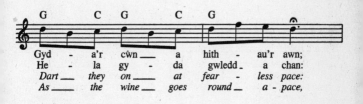

G   C   G   C   G

Gyd - a'r cŵn __ a hith - au'r awn;
He - la gy - da gwledd __ a chan:
Dart __ they on __ at fear - less pace:
As __ the wine __ goes round __ a - pace,

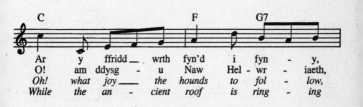

C   F   G7

Ar   y ffridd __ wrth fyn'd i fyn - y,
O!   am ddysg - u Naw Hel - wr - iaeth,
Oh!   what joy __ the hounds to fol - low,
While the an - cient roof is ring - ing

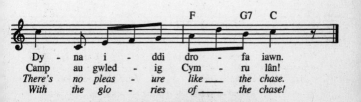

F   G7   C

Dy - na i - ddi dro - fa iawn.
Camp - au gwled - ig Cym - ru lân!
There's no pleas - ure like __ the chase.
With the glo - ries of __ the chase!

Wales
LLWYN ON
(The Ash Grove)

A

1. Yn Mhal - as Llwyn On gynt, fe
2. Rhy hwyr yd - oedd gal - w y
1. The ash grove how grace - ful, how
2. My lips smile no more, my heart

Bm/D   **E**   **A/C#**

drig - ai pen - def - ig Ef - e oedd ys -
saeth at y llwyn A'r llanc - es yn
plain - ly 'tis speak - ing, The harp through it
los - es its light - ness, No dream of the

D   **A/E**   **E7**   **A**

gwei - ar ac ar - glwydd y wlad; Ac
mar - w yn wel - w a gwan; By -
play - ing has lan - guage for me; When -
fu - ture my spir - it can cheer, I

Bm/D

idd - o un en - eth a an - wyd yn
gyth - iodd ei gledd - yf trwy gal - on y
ev - er the light through its branch - es is
on - ly would brood on the past and its

E   **A/C#**   **D**

un - ig A hi' nol yr han - es oedd
llenc - yn; Ond ni red - ai Car - iad un
break - ing, A host of kind fa - ces is
bright - ness, The dead I have mourn'd are a -

Wales

RHYFELGYRCH GWYR HARLECH

(Men of Harlech)

Words by Ceriog
Folk Melody

Well - uh goil - kairth wen un flam - yo,
See the flames of fires like hell there,

Ah thav - ode - i tahn un bloyth - yo, Ahr eer dew - rion
Fie - ry tongues that ache and swell there. Hear the brave man's

thod ee dah - ro, Een - wythe et on een.
bat - tle yell there: On - ward as we go.

Gahn - von - llev i tuh - ois - og - yon, Llice gel - on - yon,
Hear the war cries ar - mor clash - ing chief - tains urge the

troost ar - vog - yon Ah char - lom - yod uh march - og - yon,
right - eous thrash - ing, Sol - diers ride on hor - ses dash - ing,

Creig - ar grieg ah green! Ahr - von beeth nee
On - ward as we go. Ar - fon sings on

or - veeth, Ken - eer un dra - guh weeth,
al - ways, Of her might and glo - ry.

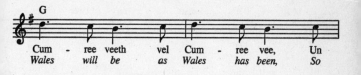

Cum - ree veeth vel Cum - ree vee, Un
Wales will be as Wales has been, So

glode - ees __ um __ mus __ gled - eeth. Ung
great __ in __ free - dom's __ sto - ry. These

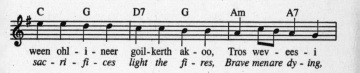

ween ohl - i - neer goil - kerth ak - oo, Tros wev - ees - i
sac - ri - fi - ces light the fi - res, Brave men are dy - ing,

Cum - rone mah - roo, On - nee - bun - yeith
Wales in - spi - res, Free - dom drives us

seeth un gal - oo, Am i day - rav deen!
ev - er high - er, Welsh-men must be free.

Wales
SOSPAN VACH
(The Little Saucepan)

GUITAR CHORD FRAMES

	C	Cm	C+	C6	Cm6
C		3fr			

	C#	C#m	C#+	C#6	C#m6
C#/Db		4fr		3fr	2fr

	D	Dm	D+	D6	Dm6
D					

	Eb	Ebm	Eb+	Eb6	Ebm6
Eb/D#	3fr				

	E	Em	E+	E6	Em6
E					

	F	Fm	F+	F6	Fm6
F					

This guitar chord reference includes 120 commonly used chords. For a more complete guide to guitar chords, see "THE PAPERBACK CHORD BOOK" (HL00702009).

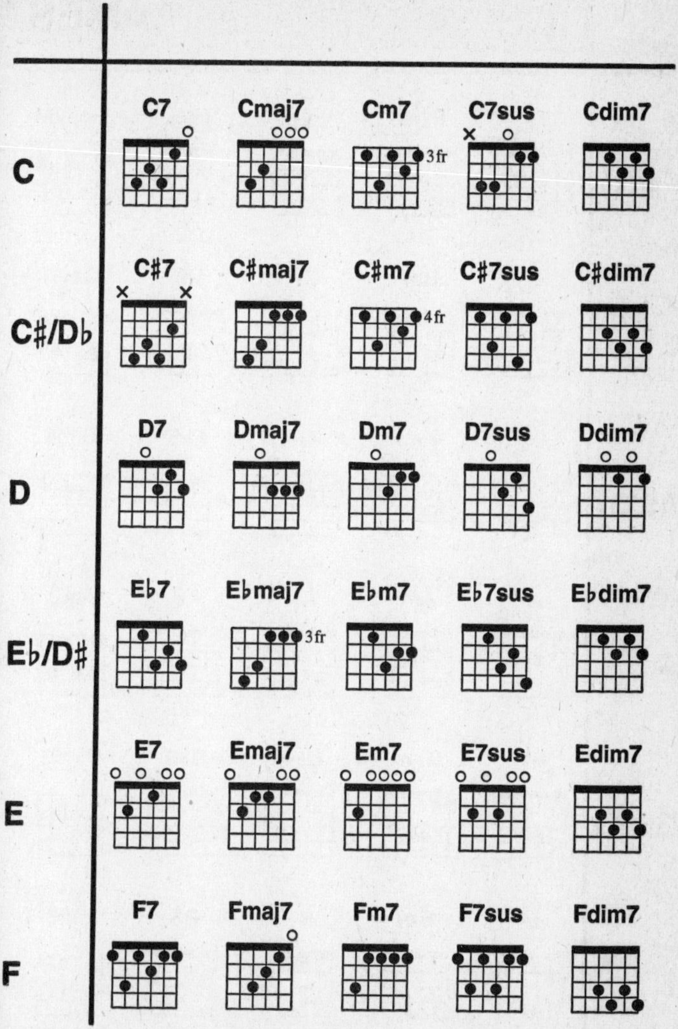
C
C7
Cmaj7
Cm7
3fr
C7sus
Cdim7
C♯/D♭
C♯7
C♯maj7
C♯m7
4fr
C♯7sus
C♯dim7
D
D7
Dmaj7
Dm7
D7sus
Ddim7
E♭/D♯
E♭7
E♭maj7
3fr
E♭m7
E♭7sus
E♭dim7
E
E7
Emaj7
Em7
E7sus
Edim7
F
F7
Fmaj7
Fm7
F7sus
Fdim7

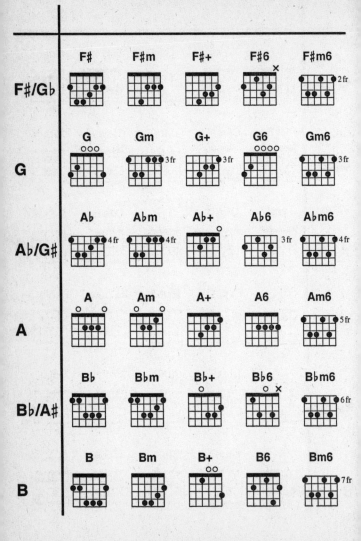

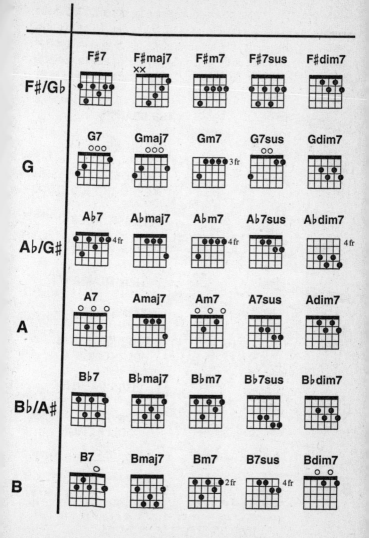

THE PAPERBACK SONGS SERIES

These perfectly portable paperbacks include the melodies, lyrics, and chords symbols for your favorite songs, all in a convenient, pocket-sized book. Using concise, one-line music notation, anyone from hobbyists to professionals can strum on the guitar, play melodies on the piano, or sing the lyrics to great songs. Books also include a helpful guitar chord chart. A fantastic deal – only $5.95 each!

THE BEATLES
00702008

THE BLUES
00702014

CHORDS FOR KEYBOARD & GUITAR
00702009

CLASSIC ROCK
00310058

COUNTRY HITS
00702013

NEIL DIAMOND
00702012

HYMNS
00240103

INTERNATIONAL FOLKSONGS
00240104

ELVIS PRESLEY
00240102

THE ROCK & ROLL COLLECTION
00702020

FOR MORE INFORMATION, SEE YOUR LOCAL MUSIC DEALER,
OR WRITE TO:

HAL•LEONARD®
CORPORATION

7777 W. BLUEMOUND RD. P.O. BOX 13819 MILWAUKEE, WI 53213